FRAGMENTS FROM DIṄNĀGA

FRAGMENTS FROM DIṄNĀGA

H. N. RANDLE

MOTILAL BANARSIDASS
Delhi :: Varanasi :: Patna

First Edition : The Royal Asiatic Society, London 1926
First Indian Reprint : Delhi 1981

ISBN: 978-81-2082-980-0

Also available at:

MOTILAL BANARSIDASS
41 U.A. Bungalow Road, Jawahar Nagar, Delhi 110 007
8 Mahalaxmi Chamber, Warden Road, Mumbai 400 026
120 Royapettah High Road, Mylapore, Chennai 600 004
Sanas Plaza, Subhash Nagar, Pune 411 002
16 St. Mark's Road, Bangalore 560 001
8 Camac Street, Calcutta 700 017
Ashok Rajpath, Patna 800 004
Chowk, Varanasi 221 0011

PRINTED IN INDIA

BY JAINENDRA PRAKASH JAIN AT SHRI JAINENDRA PRESS,
A-45 NARAINA, PHASE I, NEW DELHI 110 028
AND PUBLISHED BY NARENDRA PRAKASH JAIN FOR
MOTILAL BANARSIDASS PUBLISHERS PRIVATE LIMITED,
BUNGALOW ROAD, DELHI 110 007

PREFACE

This treatise was originally written as part of a study of *Indian Logic in the Early Schools* undertaken for the doctorate in Philosophy of the University of Oxford. Dr. F. W. Thomas, to whom I am greatly indebted for his encouragement and assistance, suggested its separate publication; and my thanks are due to the Council of the Royal Asiatic Society for deciding to publish it as a monograph. I desire also to express my gratitude to Mr. A. H. Mackenzie, Director of Public Instruction, United Provinces, and to the United Provinces Government, for the grant of study leave which has enabled me to carry out the work.

H. N. RANDLE.

July, 1926.

CONTENTS

LIST OF FRAGMENTS

[**Fragments asterisked have been identified by Vidyābhūṣaṇa in the Tibetan version of *Pramāṇa-samuccaya*.**]

Fragment.	*Source.*
*A. Definition of Perception . . .	*NV*, p. 44, l. 1, and *NVT*, p. 102, l. 10.
*B. The 'internal organ' . . .	*NVT*, p. 97, ll. 1 and 28.
C. Difficulty as to the visual organ's being in contact with its object (4 lines) .	*NVT*, p. 76, l. 28.
D. How can substance be seen if only colour is the object of vision ? (prose citation)	*NVT*, p. 129, l. 22.
*E. Testimony not a separate source of knowledge	*NV*, p. 63, l. 13; *NVT*, p. 138, l. 19.
*F. What is the *probandum* in inference ? (8 lines)	*NVT*, p. 120, l. 12.
G. Definition of *anumāna* or the instrument of inferential knowledge . .	*NV*, p. 56, l. 14.
*H. The three characters of a valid reason or middle term . . .	*NV*, p. 58, l. 2.
I. (i) Inference for another; (ii) proof .	*NRA*, p. 252 and p. 250.
*J. The nine reasons or types of argument (8 lines)	*NVT*, p. 198, l. 1.
K. *All* middle terms are *pakṣa-dharma* .	*NVT*, p. 198, l. 14; cf. *NV*, p. 132, l. 13.
L. Criticism of the definition of *hetu* given in *NS*, I, i, 34 (4½ lines) . .	*NVT*, pp. 189-190 (p. 189, l. 16 to p. 190, l. 2); *NV*, p. 123, l. 8 to p. 125, l. 4.
M. Definition of *hetu* . . .	*NV*, p. 134, l. 13.
N. 'Comparison' as a source of knowledge is reducible to perception or testimony	*NVT*, p. 135, l. 14; cf. *NV*, p. 60, l. 16.
O. The object of inference is merely an ideal construction (prose citation) . .	*NVT*, p. 127, l. 1; p. 39, l. 13; cf. *Śl. Vārt.*, *nirālambana*, verses 167-168.
P. Definition of *vāda* . .	*NV*, p. 124, l. 8; cf. *NV*, p. 151, l. 20, and *NVT*, p. 218, l. 9.

Fragment.	*Source.*
Q. Criticism of the *Vaiśeṣika* account of the universal (*sāmānya*) (6 lines) . .	*SDS*, chapter on *Bauddhas*, p. 22= Cowell and Gough, p. 21.

Note.—All these fragments are definitely attributed to Diṅnāga by Vācaspati Miśra except fragments P and Q. Fragment Q is attributed to Diṅnāga on the authority of a *Jaina* logician who cites two of the lines as Diṅnāga's: and there seems to be no reason to doubt the attribution. Vidyābhūṣaṇa has identified six of these fragments with passages from the Tibetan version of the *Pramāṇa-samuccaya*, as follows:

A=*Pramāṇa-samuccaya*, Chapter I (*HIL*, p. 277).
B= ,, ,, ,, I (p. 280).
E= ,, ,, ,, II (p. 288).
F= ,, ,, ,, II (p. 281).
H= ,, ,, ,, II (p. 288).
J= ,, ,, ,, III (p. 283).

For the attribution of fragment Q to Diṅnāga, see Vidyābhūṣaṇa, *HIL*, p. 273.

The arrangement of the fragments here follows what seems to be the probable order of the topics in the *Pramāṇa-samuccaya*.

Thus: A, B, C, D=Chapter I (perception).
E, F, G, H=Chapter II (inference for oneself).
J, K (L, M ?)=Chapter III (inference for another).
(L, M,) N=Chapter IV (reason and example).
Q=Chapter V (apoha).
O and P can hardly be located.

BIBLIOGRAPHY OF WORKS REFERRED TO, AND ABBREVIATIONS USED IN CITING CERTAIN WORKS

Faddegon, B. *The Vaiśeṣika System described with the help of the oldest texts.* Amsterdam, 1918.

Jhā, Gaṅganātha. *Translation of the Nyāya-sūtra, Nyāya-bhāṣya, and Nyāya-vārttika. Indian Thought*, Allahabad, 1910-1920; and separately.

Jhā, Gaṅganātha. *PSPM=Prābhākara School of Pūrva Mīmāṁsā.* Allahabad, 1911; and in *Indian Thought.*

Keith, A. B. *BP=Buddhist Philosophy in India and Ceylon.* Oxford University Press, 1923.

Keith, A. B. *ILA=Indian Logic and Atomism, an exposition of the Nyāya and Vaiśeṣika systems.* Oxford University Press, 1921.

NBh=Nyāya-bhāṣya of Vātsyāyana, edited with the *Sūtra* and with extracts from the *Vārttika* and the *Tātparya-ṭīkā*, by Gaṅgādhara Śāstrī Tailaṅga. *Vizianagram Sanskrit Series*, Benares, 1896.

References are to this edition. It has also been edited with the *Sūtra* and the *Vṛtti* by Lakṣmaṇa Śāstrī and Rāma Śāstrī, Benares, 1920.

NK=Nyāya-kandalī of Śrīdhara Miśra, on Praśastapāda's *bhāṣya*, with which it is edited.

NRA=Nyāya-ratnākara of Pārthasārathi Miśra, on Kumārila's *Śloka-vārttika*, with which it is edited.

NS=Nyāya-sūtra. Printed with editions of the *Nyāya-bhāṣya* and *Nyāya-vārttika.* Edited and translated by S. C. Vidyābhūṣaṇa, in the *Sacred Books of the Hindus Series*, Allahabad, 1909.

NV=Nyāya-vārttika of Uddyotakara. Edited by Vindhyeśvari Prasāda Dvivedi (Dūbe), *Bibliotheca Indica*, Calcutta, 1907. References are to this edition. A later and in some respects better edition is that by the same editor and Lakṣmaṇa Śāstrī Draviḍa in the *Chowkhamba Sanskrit Series*, Benares, 1915.

NVT=Nyāya-vārttika-tātparya-ṭīkā (briefly *Tātparya-ṭīkā*) of Vācaspati Miśra. Edited by Gaṅgādhara Śāstrī Tailaṅga, *Vizianagram Sanskrit Series*, Benares, 1898. References are to this edition. It is now being edited by Śrirājeśvara Śāstrī Draviḍa in the *Benares Sanskrit Series.* (The first *adhyāya* only has appeared so far, in 1925. It is a very valuable check on the earlier edition.)

PBh = Praśastapāda's *Bhāṣya* on the *Vaiśeṣika* system. Sometimes called the *Padārtha-dharma-saṁgraha*. Edited, with the *Nyāya-kandalī*, by Vindhyeśvari Prasāda Dvivedi, *Vizianagram Sanskrit Series*, Benares, 1895.

Péri, Noël. *À propos de la date de Vasubandhu*. In *Bulletin de l'École Française de l'Extrême-Orient*, xi, 1911.

SDS = *Sarva-darśana-saṁgraha* of Mādhava. There have been many editions since the *Bibliotheca Indica* edition of 1858. As the edition which I have used is not accessible, I have given references to the translation by E. B. Cowell and A. E. Gough, *Trübner's Oriental Series*, 2nd edition, 1894. The chapter on the *Bauddha* system has been translated by L. de la Vallée Poussin (with very valuable notes) in *le Muséon*, n.s. ii, 1901, under the title *Le Bouddhisme d'après les sources brahmaniques.*

Stcherbatsky, Th. (1) *Rapports entre la théorie bouddhique de la connaissance et l'enseignement des autres écoles philosophiques de l'Inde*. In *le Muséon*, n.s. v, 1904.

(2) *Epistemology and Logic of the Later Buddhist Schools* (in Russian), St. Petersburg, 1911. A communication from Stcherbatsky in English, summarising some of his then views, is given in Jacobi's article on the *Dates of the Philosophical Sūtras*, *Journal of the American Oriental Society*, xxxi, 1911. The work has now been translated into German, *Erkenntnistheorie u. Logik nach der Lehre der späteren Buddhisten*, O. Strauss, München-Neubiberg, 1924. The translation contains an important appendix (p. 259) stating Stcherbatsky's very much modified present views.

Sugiura, Sadajiro. *Hindu Logic as preserved in China and Japan.* Philadelphia, 1900. (The author apparently knew no Sanskrit, and was not acquainted with the logic of the orthodox schools. But he gives very valuable information.)

Śl. Vārt. = *Śloka-vārttika* of Kumārila Bhaṭṭa on the *tarka-pāda* of Śabara's *Bhāṣya* on the *Mīmāṁsā*. Edited, together with the *Nyāya-ratnākara* of Pārthasārathi Miśra, by Rāma Śāstrī Tailaṅga, *Chowkhamba Sanskrit Series*, Benares, 1898-1899. Translated by Gaṅganātha Jhā, *Bibliotheca Indica*, Calcutta, 1900-1908.

Ui, H. *Vaiśeṣika Philosophy according to the Daśapadārtha-śāstra*, Royal Asiatic Society, London, 1918.

VS = *Vaiśeṣika-sūtra*. Edited and translated by A. E. Gough, Benares, 1873 (reprint from *The Pandit*); and by Nand Lāl Sinha, *Sacred Books of the Hindus*, Allahabad, 1911. There was a *Bibliotheca Indica* edition, with the *Upaskāra* of Śaṁkara Miśra, Calcutta, 1861.

Vidyābhūṣaṇa, Satis Candra. (1) *MSIL* = *Indian Logic Mediæval School*, Calcutta University, 1909. This is embodied in a revised form in—

(2) *HIL* = *History of Indian Logic Ancient Mediæval and Modern School*. Calcutta University, 1922. See notice in *J.R.A.S*, April, 1925, pp. 345-348.

ERRATA

Page 1, note 3: for *Trikāla-parīkṣa* read *°kṣā*.
Page 3, note 2: for *sahādhyayaḥ* read *sahādhyāyaḥ*.
Page 3, note 2: for *Adreḥ sṛṅgaṁ* read *°śṛṅgaṁ*.
Page 9, line 14: for *nāmajāti-yojānā* read *°yojanā*.
Page 12, line 4: for *yogacāra* read *yogācāra*.
Page 12, line 10: for *yogācara* read *yogācāra*.
Page 16, note 1: for *saktir* read *śaktir*.
Page 19, line 3: for *srūyeta* read *śrūyeta*.
Page 21, line 19: for *nāntarīyakas* read *°kaś*.
Page 21, line 20: for *tav-vido . . . tam* read *tad-vido . . taṁ*.
Page 24, note 1: *for* I, i, 5 *read* I, i, 34.
Page 25, lines 14-15: for *parārthānumana* read *°māna*.
Page 25, line 29: for *teṣām* read *teṣāṁ*.
Page 27, note 1: for *svaṛūpenaiva* read *svarūpeṇaiva*.
Page 27, last line: for *svarūpenaiva* read *svarūpeṇaiva*.
Page 30, line 7: for *dvedha* read *°dhā*.
Page 30, line 13: for *śāsvatāḥ* read *śāśvatāḥ*.
Page 34, line 3: for *uktam* read *uktaṁ*.
Page 34, last line but one: for *kenaital* read *°tal*.
Page 36, line 7: for *udāharaṇā* read *°ṇa*.
Page 37, note 1: for *pancamī* read *pañcamī*.
Page 37, note 2: for *-avyabhichāritvād* read *°cāritvād*.
Page 39, line 2: for *prakārakatvam* read *°tvaṁ*.
Page 41, note 1: for *lakṣaṇam* read *°ṇaṁ*.
Page 42, line 18: for *viśeṣyam . . . evārthad* read *viśeṣyaṁ . . . evārthād*.
Page 42, line 19: for *kutah* read *kutaḥ*.
Page 46, line 5: for *prabandum* read *pro°*.
Page 49, line 16: for *vakyād* read *vākyād*.
Page 50, line 25: for *vakyād* read *vākyād*.
Page 51, line 12: for *upasaṁharāt* read *°hārāt*.
Page 51, line 20: for *yan nāntarīyakaṁ* read *yannā°*.
Page 51, line 26: for *yadā 'hur* read *yad āhur*.
Page 51, line 31: for *Śloka-vārtika* read *°vārttika*.
Page 52, line 6: for *'numananumeya* read *'numānānumeya*.

Page 53, line 13: for *samvṛti* read *saṁvṛti*.
Page 54, last line: for *svābhimatam* read °*taṁ*.
Page 62, line 8 from end: for *Vaiśesika* read °*sika*.
Page 63, line 8 from end: *for* is sound *read* of sound.
Page 67, line 14: *for* it *read* the doctrine.
Page 68, line 9: for *samyoga* read *saṁ*°.
Page 70, line 7: for *lingāsiddha* read *liṅgā*°.

Page 78, for lines 5-10 substitute:

vipakṣāvṛtti, where M is a peculiar property of S, found neither in positive nor in negative instances) holds a special position and is called *asādhāraṇa*.[1] Uddyotakara argues in the first place that an *asādhāraṇa-dharma* or peculiar property of S may be a valid reason if there *are* no instances of XP; and he points out in the second place that the example

Page 80, line 1: *for* similar cases *read* other instances of M.

INDEX.

Page 85, column 1, line 23: for *sāmanya* read *sāmānya*.
Page 85, column 2, lines 20-21: for *pañcāvāyava* read °*vayava*.
Page 85, column 2, line 36: *after* 25 *insert* 82.
Page 86, column 1, lines 28-29: for *avāyava* read *ava*°.
Page 88, column 1, line 18: transfer *aprāmāṇya* so as to precede *abhidhāna*.
Page 88, column 1, line 46: *for* Asanga *read* Asaṅga.
Page 88, column 2, line 10: for *āptodeśa* read *āptoddeśa*.
Page 89, column 1, line 33: for *kṣana* read *kṣaṇa*.
Page 89, column 2, lines 35-37: transfer so as to follow *dharma*.
Page 89, column 2, lines 54-56: transfer so as to follow *nigamana* on p. 90.
Page 90, column 2, line 2 from end: transfer so as to follow *manas*.
Page 91, column 1, line 47: for *vijñānā-vāda* read *vijñāna-vāda*.
Page 91, column 2, line 41: *before* 31 *insert* 23.
Page 92, column 1, line 4: for *sajatīya* read *sajātīya*.
Page 92, column 1, line 42: for *samyoga* read *saṁyoga*.

INTERPRETATION OF LOGICAL FRAGMENTS FROM DIṄNĀGA

Diṅnāgānāṁ pathi pariharan sthūla-hastāvalepān

(Kālidāsa's *Megha-dūta*, I, 14).

FRAGMENTS FROM DINNĀGA

SECTION 1.—INTRODUCTORY.

Vācaspati Miśra states that Uddyotakara's motive in composing the *Nyāya-vārttika* was to remove the obscurity in which the *śāstra* had become veiled owing to the misinterpretations of Diṅnāga and others.[1] This statement is fully borne out both by the contents of the *Vārttika* itself and by the numerous citations which Vācaspati fortunately makes from Diṅnāga. Certain of these citations have been identified by Vidyābhūṣaṇa[2] with passages in the Tibetan version of the *Pramāṇa-samuccaya*, which is one of the works attributed to Diṅnāga in the Tanjur.[3] Not one of them has been

[1] *NVT*, p. 1, l. 14. *Dinnāga-prabhṛtibhir arvācīnaiḥ kuhetu-santamasa-samutthāpanenāvacchaditaṁ śāstram . . . ity Uddyotakareṇa svanibandhoddyotena tad apanīyate.*

Uddyotakara himself says in the introductory verses attached to the *Vārttika:*

yad Akṣapādaḥ pravaro munīnām
śamāya śāstraṁ jagato jagāda
kutārkikājñāna-nivṛtti-hetuḥ
kariṣyate tasya mayā nibandhaḥ.

[2] S. C. Vidyābhūṣaṇa, *History of Indian Logic*, Calcutta, 1921), pp. 273-288 footnotes. The central part of this work deals with 'the Mediæval School,' and is a revised version of the account given in his *Indian Logic Mediæval School* (Calcutta, 1909). The later version corrects in important points the earlier.

[3] Besides the *Pramāṇa-samuccaya*, Diṅnāga is the reputed author of the following works which are extant in Chinese and Tibetan versions:

(i) *Pramāṇa-samuccaya-vṛtti.*

(ii) *Ālambana-parīkṣā.*

(iii) *Ālambana-parīkṣā-vṛtti.*

(iv) *Trikāla-parīkṣa.*

(v) And a strictly logical work with regard to the exact title and contents of which it would seem that the Tibetan and the Chinese

identified with any passage from any other of the works there attributed to Diṅnāga. While therefore we have in the *Nyāya-vārttika-tātparya-ṭīkā* evidence which amounts to proof that the *Pramāṇa-samuccaya* is the work of Diṅnāga, we have complete absence of such evidence in the case of the *Nyāya-praveśa*,[1] the other logical work attributed to him.

Diṅnāga's date falls somewhere between the date of the *Nyāya-bhāṣya*, which he criticises, and that of Uddyotakara, who replies to his criticism. Uddyotakara may be taken with considerable probability to have flourished in the early years of the seventh century. Vātsyāyana's date may be approximately 300 A.D. Diṅnāga is said to have been a disciple of Vasubandhu, whose date, however, is "not yet quite settled":[2] but the earliest computation puts his death at

---

traditions are at variance. *Cf.* Ui's *Vaiśeṣika Philosophy*, p. 68 footnote, with Vidyābhūṣaṇa's *History of Indian Logic*, p. 289 footnote, 300 footnote, and 302 with footnotes. It is, I think, impossible to accept the accuracy of Vidyābhūṣaṇa's statements without assuming that the Tibetan tradition is at variance with the Chinese. Vidyābhūṣaṇa says that the *Nyāya-praveśa* of which he gives a detailed account is ascribed in the Tanjur to Diṅnāga. Ui says that his account corresponds (not, as Vidyābhūṣaṇa asserts, to Nos. 1223 and 1224 of the Chinese Tripiṭaka, which purport to be two distinct Chinese versions of a *Nyāya-dvāra* ascribed to Diṅnāga, but) to No. 1216—the *Hetu-vidyā-nyāya-praveśa-śāstra* ascribed to one Śaṁkara Svāmin, a disciple of Diṅnāga (who, according to Vidyābhūṣaṇa, is unknown to Tibetan tradition). Vidyābhūṣaṇa suggests a doubt as to whether the original Sanskrit of 1216 was different from that of 1224 (and of 1223): but Sugiura's account shows that the two works are quite distinct.

The Gaekwad's Oriental Series advertises as in the press a "*Nyāya-praveśa* of Diṅnāga," which will doubtless prove to be the Sanskrit original of the work of which Vidyābhūṣaṇa gives an account.

[1] As regards the '*Hetu-cakra-hamaru*' which Vidyābhūṣaṇa at first treated as a separate work of Diṅnāga, he now says that it is a chapter of the '*Nyāya-praveśa*.' The title should no doubt be *Hetu-cakra-ḍamaru* (as suggested by Dr. F. W. Thomas—agreeing with Cordier): but Dr. Thomas states that the block-print actually has *-hamaru*.

[2] Stcherbatsky, *Central Conception of Buddhism*, p. 2, n. 2. "The dates of the Chinese translations of the works of Asanga and Vasubandhu, if correct, would be sufficient evidence to assign them to the fourth century. Otherwise one feels inclined to bring Vasubandhu nearer to Diṅnāga, whose teacher he was." Keith, *B.P.*, p. 155, inclines

350 A.D. The indication of Diṅnāga's date afforded by the fact that two of the works attributed to him were translated into Chinese in 557 and 569 A.D.[1] carries us a little further. But the supposed reference to him as a contemporary in Kālidāsa's *Megha-dūta*[2] can hardly be regarded as evidence. All that can be said with certainty is that he lived somewhere between 350 A.D. and 500 A.D.

It does not seem feasible, in this uncertainty, to argue from absolute to relative chronology. Except in those rare cases in which an author dates his own works (and dates them in an era that can be identified), the safest procedure would seem to be to attempt to fix the relative chronology of works on

---

to Péri's view that Vasubandhu's death was not later than 350 A.D. On the strength of this he suggsts in *ILA*, p. 98, that Diṅnāga may have flourished before 400 A.D.

[1] Vidyābhūṣaṇa, *HIL*, p. 272. Vidyābhūṣaṇa's dating of Diṅnāga as 'about 500 A.D.' depends on his dating of Vasubandhu about 480 A.D.

[2] See Mallinātha's comment on *Megha-dūta*, I, 14. There is nothing in Kālidāsa's lines to suggest the secondary meaning which Mallinātha reads into them. He says the reference in *sarasaniculād* is to a *rasiko Niculo nāma mahākaviḥ, Kalidāsasya sahādhyayaḥ, parāpāditānāṁ Kālidāsa-prabandha-dūṣaṇānāṁ parihartā*; and he explains *diṅnāgānāṁ* as *Diṅnāgācāryasya Kālidāsa-pratipakṣasya*. The title *-ācāryasya* suggests the famous Buddhist: otherwise it might be supposed that Mallinātha had some other Diṅnāga, poet or literary critic, in view: for the notion of the *logician* Diṅnāga in the rôle of literary critic here assigned to him does not carry conviction.

Kālidāsa's lines are:

Adreḥ sṛṅgaṁ harati pavanaḥ kiṁsvid ity unmukhībhir
Dṛṣṭotsāhaś cakita-cakitaṁ mugdha-siddhāṅganābhiḥ
Sthānād asmād sarasa-niculād utpatodaṅmukhaṁ khaṁ
Diṅnāgānām pathi pariharan sthūla-hastāvalepān.

Mallinātha did not *invent* the secondary meaning suggested: his comment embodies a tradition. Nevertheless, its value as evidence for the date of the great Diṅnāga would still be small, even if Kālidāsa's date were more certain than it is. See, however, F. W. Thomas in *J.R.A.S.*, January, 1918, pp. 118-122. Kṣetreśacandra Chaṭṭopādhyāya, in an article on the Date of Kālidāsa (Allahabad University Studies, Vol. II, 1926), points out that the earliest commentators on the *Megha-dūta* do not read any secondary meaning into these lines. This suggests that the supposed reference to Diṅnāga is a later invention.

the basis of internal evidence. The immediate application of this remark is to the difficult problem of the relation of Diṅnāga to Praśastapāda. The absolute date of Praśastapāda is even more uncertain than the absolute date of Diṅnāga: and it is not therefore possible to settle the question of indebtedness by a consideration of priority. It is a question which can be settled only by internal evidence; and until it has been settled beyond reasonable possibility of doubt, it should not be permitted either to affect, or to be affected by, the chronological issue.[1]

In any attempt to fix the relation of Diṅnāga to Praśastapāda it is essential to argue from doctrines which are indubitably Diṅnāga's. It is also very desirable to have these doctrines in his own words, since the cogency of a conclusion may turn on the word which a writer uses and on the precise shade of meaning which it has for him. Of the two logical works attributed to Diṅnāga, the *Nyāya-praveśa* satisfies neither of these two conditions.[2] An account of it has been given by Vidyābhūṣaṇa in his *History of Indian Logic;* but for the reasons indicated it does not furnish data which can safely be used for purposes of instituting a comparison between the logic of Diṅnāga and that of Praśastapāda.

The case is quite different with the *Pramāṇa-samuccaya.*

[1] *Cf.* Keith, *ILA*, p. 27 and p. 99. "The upper limit of date is suggested by Praśastapāda's indebtedness to Diṅnāga, whose most probable date is about 400 A.D., and it would accord well enough with all probability if Praśastapāda were referred to the fifth century." "It is clear that so far as chronological grounds go there is nothing to prevent the supposition that Praśastapāda was indebted for his system largely to Diṅnāga." There is also nothing to prevent the supposition that Diṅnāga was indebted to Praśastapāda. Stcherbatsky now (1924) has accepted this supposition, and maintains that Praśastapāda was either a contemporary or a predecessor of Vasubandhu, the teacher of Diṅnāga. See his Appendix contributed to the German translation of his *Epistemology and Logic according to the Later Buddhists* (1909, St. Petersburg), translated into German by Strauss (1924, Munich).

[2] To use the much later *Nyāya-bindu* as authority for Diṅnāga's doctrine is obviously very precarious. For the *Nyāya-praveśa* see note above.

It is indubitably the work of Diṅnāga. And considerable fragments of it, and these from the nature of the case dealing with important aspects of his doctrine, are accessible in his own words, as quoted by Vācaspati Miśra. Under these circumstances it seems useful to collect and interpret the various citations from the *Pramāṇa-samuccaya* embodied in the *Nyāya-vārttika-tātparya-ṭīkā*, together with the meagre fragments to be found here and there in the *Vārttika*.[1] Stcherbatsky[2] in fact relied largely upon these quotations: and there is at present no other safe method of approach to the understanding of Diṅnāga's teaching. This study is therefore devoted to an attempt to interpret these fragments of the *Pramāṇa-samuccaya*, fitting them so far as possible into the general framework of the *Pramāṇa-samuccaya* as outlined in Vidyābhūṣaṇa's *History of Indian Logic*. The arrangement of the topics in that work seems to have been as follows, when Vidyābhūṣaṇa's somewhat confused account[3] is interpreted and supplemented in the light of the references which he himself gives.

[1] It is not Uddyotakara's habit to quote. He was not a scholar like Vācaspati Miśra, and contents himself with the merest scraps of citation (though by a happy chance he gives us, on one occasion, a couple of lines from the Buddhist *Sūtra of the Burden-bearer*—*N V*, p. 342, l. 3).

[2] In *le Muséon*, n.s. vol. v, 1904. *Rapports entre la théorie Bouddhique da la connaissance et l'enseignement des autres écoles philosophiques des Indes.*

[3] The account is not clear as regards the latter three of the six chapters into which the work is divided: and the account given of these three chapters in the *History of Indian Logic* differs from the account given in *Mediæval School of Indian Logic*.

Chapter I.—*Perception.*

Chapter II.—*Inference for oneself.*

Chapter III.—*Inference for another.*

(Account in *MSIL*) Chapter IV.—*Three characteristics of the middle term* (probably the end of Chapter III; see *HIL*): and *rejection of comparison.*

(Account in *HIL*) Chapter IV.—*Reason and example.*

(Account in *MSIL*) Chapter V.—*Rejection of Verbal Testimony.*

(Account in *HIL*) Chapter V.—*Apoha.* This is given as the general heading. But the following topics appear to be treated as belonging to this chapter:

SECTION 2.—PROBABLE ARRANGEMENT OF TOPICS IN DIṄNĀGA'S '*Pramāṇa-samuccaya.*'

Chapter I.—Perception (=*NS*, I, i, 4).

(i) There are only two *pramāṇas*, viz. perception and inference.

(ii) Characterisation of Perception.

(iii) Criticism of the definitions of perception given by (*a*) the *Yogācāras*, (*b*) the *Sāṁkhyas*, (*c*) the *Naiyāyikas*. The *Naiyāyikas*' importation of *manas* as an *indriya* from the *Vaiśeṣikas*. The *indriyatva* of *manas* connected with the question of the *prameyatva* of the qualities of *atma*, i.e. *sukhādi*. Failure of the *Naiyāyika* to provide a place in their account of *saṁnikarṣa* for the five '*viśeṣaṇas*' which are an essential part of the *Vaiśeṣika* theory.

Chapter II.—Inference for oneself (=*NS*, I, i, 5).

(i) Defined as knowledge derived through a mark of three kinds.

(ii) The three kinds are (*a*) *kārya*, (*b*) *svabhāva*, (*c*) *anupalabdhi*.

[1][(iii) *śabda-pramāṇa* is a case of *anumāna* (=*NS*, I, i, 7).]

(iv) What is the *probandum* (*anumeya*) of the inference ?

Comparison.—A line is quoted in this connection as from Chapter IV, however.

Verbal Testimony.—One of the citations given in this connection is quoted as from Chapter II. The citation in question says that verbal testimony is included in perception and *inference*.

Law governing the middle term.—Here is quoted the well-known statement of the *trairūpya* —*anumeye 'tha tattulye sadbhāvo nāstitā 'sati*— but it is quoted as from Chapter II.

(Account in *MSIL*) Chapter VI.—*Barts of a syllogism.* (Chapter heading only given, on p. 85. No account at all is given of this chapter on p. 88 in connection with the accounts of the other chapters. It may be regarded as a mistake.)

(Account in *HIL*) Chapter VI.—*Analogue*, i.e. *jāti*.

[1] Position here conjectural. Vidyābhūṣaṇa puts this under V (iii) *infra*, but the quotation he gives is from this chapter.

[(v) The instrument (*anumāna*) of *svārthānumiti* defined as *nāntariyakārtha-darśanaṁ tadvidaḥ.*]

[1][(vi) The *trairūpya —anumeye'tha tattulye sadbhāvo nāstitā 'sati.*]

Chapter III.—Inference for another.

(i) Defined.

(ii) *sādhya* [or *pratijñā* (?)] defined.

" Diṅnāga reviews the definitions of a proposition as given by Akṣapāda and the *Mīmāṁsaka.*"

(iii) Formal logic of the *trairūpya.* Valid and invalid reason. The nine types of inference. [*paksa-dharmatā* the common characteristic both of the *hetu* and of the *hetvābhāsa.*]

Chapter IV.—*Hetu* and *Udāharaṇa* (=*NS*, I, i, 34-37).

(i) [Criticism of the definition of *hetu* in *NS*, I, i, 34.]

Affirmative and Negative Reason. Affirmative and Negative Example.

[(ii) *Grāhya-dharmas tad-aṁśena vyāpto hetuḥ.*]

[(iii) *Upamāna* as inference. Criticism of Vātsyāyana's interpretation of *NS*, I, i, 6.]

Chapter V.—Apoha.

(i) The six categories of the *Vaiśeṣika* [in the light of the *apoha-vāda.* Refutation of the *Vaiśeṣika* doctrine of *sāmānya*].

(ii) [Discussion of *sādṛśya.*] *Upamāna* as knowledge of *sādṛśya* [which may become the ground of an *inference*—see Chapter IV (iii) in this list of topics] is reducible either to perception [or testimony].

(iii) *śabda* [in the light of the *apohavāda* (for the statement that *śabdapramāṇa* is *anumāna* see Chapter II (iii) in this list of topics)].

(iv) The *trairūpya* [in the light of the *apohavāda* (*i.e.*, perhaps, the '*avadhāranas*' implied in the statement of the *trairūpya*)].

[1] Vidyābhūṣaṇa puts this under V (iv) *infra*, but the quotation is from this chapter.

Chapter VI.—Jāti (=*NS*, *Adhyāya* V).

Statement of 14 *jāti*.

Note.—The above 'list of contents' to the *Pramāṇa-samuccaya* is in part conjectural, and goes beyond Vidyābhūṣaṇa's statements. I have indicated what is conjectural, or goes beyond Vidyābhūṣaṇa's statements, by the use of square brackets. Conjecture may seem out of place when the Tibetan version is physically accessible. But Vidyābhūṣaṇa's account is the only form in which the Tibetan version is as yet intellectually accessible—except to a very few Tibetan scholars.

SECTION 3.—**Fragment A**: DEFINITION OF PERCEPTION.

(i) PRATYAKṢAṀ KALPANĀPOḌHAM.

NV, p. 44, l. 1. *apare tu manyante pratyakṣaṁ kalpanāpoḍham iti.*

NVT, p. 102, l. 1 (commenting on the above): *samprati Diṅnāgasya lakṣaṇam upanyasyati*, APARA *iti*. Later on Vācaspati draws a distinction between the view of Diṅnāga and that of Dharmakīrti:

NVT, p. 102, l. 17. *na hi yathā samyag-jñānam adhikṛtya pratyakṣādi-lakṣaṇaṁ kṛtaṁ Kīrtinā tathā Diṅnāgena, yenādhikārāj jñāne vyavatiṣṭheta kalpanāpoḍham iti bhāvaḥ.* That is, Diṅnāga does not give this definition in connection with a general rubric of 'right apprehension,' as Dharmakīrti does: and so the phrase *kalpanāpoḍham* is not fixed by the context as referring to *knowledge*—as is the case in Dharmakīrti's work. Therefore Diṅnāga is fairly open to the criticism urged in the *Vārttika*, p. 44, l. 17: *sarve arthāḥ tarhi pratyakṣāḥ prāpnuvanti.*[1]

[1] Uddyotakara has interpreted *kalpanāpoḍham* to mean *svarūpato na vyapadeśyam*—no account can be given of it as *ding-an-sich*. But this applies to *everything*—so that *everything* will be *pratyakṣa*. This consequence is avoided if we make it clear, as Dharmakīrti does, that *pratyakṣam* means *pratyakṣaṁ jñānam*. (*pratyakṣá* is subject to the ambiguity of the term 'perception,' and may refer either to the object

(ii) The explanation of the definition which Uddyotakara gives is a partial citation, and seems to be a citation from Diṅnāga:

NV, p. 44, l. 2. *atha keyaṁ kalpanā? nāma-jāti-yojaneti. yat kila na nāmnābhidhīyate na ca jātyādibhir vyapadiśyate*

VIṢAYA-SVARŪPĀNUVIDHĀYI PARICCHEDAKAM ĀTMA-SAṀVEDYAM Fragment.

tat pratyakṣam iti.

The 'fiction of the understanding' consists in joining name and class to the thing. Perception is what is not designated by a name nor expressed by class-character, etc., "a self-conscious process which determines the object and conforms to the unique individual nature of the object."[1]

(iii) Vācaspati Miśra says that the words *nāmajāti-yojānā*, etc., in the passage just cited give the answer, of the person who states the definition, to Uddyotakara's question: 'What is this *kalpanā?*' (*NVT*, p. 102, l. 2. *lakṣaṇa-vādina uttaram*). The *lakṣaṇa-vādin* seems to mean Diṅnāga, though it might mean any person who supports the definition. If it is Diṅnāga that is meant here, then the line cited just below is an additional fragment of Diṅnāga:

NVT, p. 102, l. 9. *ātmasaṁvedyam—svasaṁvedanād eva tasya kalpanā-rahitatvam*[2] *api. yathāha.*

PRATYAKṢAM KALPANĀPOḌHAM PRATYAKṢEṆAIVA SIDDHYATĪ *ti.* Fragment.

"It is just from the fact that the perception is conscious of itself that it is also known as devoid of ideal

perceived or to the perceptual *apprehension* as such.) I suppose it is avoided because *kalpanāpoḍha* could not then bear the interpretation suggested: it would mean apprehension which does not determine its object by way of *kalpanā*—not an apprehended *object* stripped of determinations.

[1] Cf. *NK*, p. 190, ll. 5-6, and p. 191, ll. 23-24. Also *SDS*, p. 36 = Cowell and Gough, p. 33.

[2] This is the reading of the Benares 1925 text. The older text mistakenly reads *kalpanāhitatvam*.

elements. As he puts it: 'It is through the perception itself that perception devoid of thought-determinations is proved.'"[1]

Section 4.—Note to Fragment A: Vasubandhu's Definition of Perception.

NV, p. 42, l. 15. *apare punar varṇayanti—*

TATO 'RTHĀD VIJÑĀNAṀ PRATYAKṢAM *iti.*

NVT, p. 99, l. 13. *tad evaṁ pratyakṣa-lakṣaṇaṁ samarthya Vāsubandhavaṁ tāvat pratyakṣa-lakṣaṇaṁ vikalpayitum upanyasyati.*

That is: Uddyotakara says:

"Some again say: 'Perception is knowledge arising from that (very) thing.'"

Vācaspati comments:

"Having thus established this (the *Naiyāyika*) definition of perception, he now cites the definition given by Vasubandhu in order to reduce it to a dilemma."

Uddyotakara explains the definition thus:

"Perception is that knowledge which arises from just that thing of which it is designated as the knowledge; and not from anything else" (*yasyārthasya yad vijñānaṁ vyapadiśyate, yadi tata eva tad bhavati nārthāntarād bhavati, tat pratyakṣam*). His criticism (*NV*, p. 42, l. 15, and p. 43, last line) contains two interesting things. One is a statement that the definition had been interpreted[2] as excluding *samvṛti-jñāna*, *i.e.* the 'fictions of the understanding' with which the 'pure

[1] This is apparently an expression of the *Bauddha* theory that cognition carries self-awareness along with it—as against the *Naiyāyika* view that we recognise our own cognitions by inner-sense perception or *mānasa-pratyakṣa*. On the *Naiyāyika* view the existence of *nirvikalpaka-jñāna* is only known by *inference*, not being open to introspection (*mānasa-pratyakṣa*).

[2] There is nothing in what Uddyotakara says which need imply that Vasubandhu himself so interpreted it. He may have done so. But equally it may have been Diṅnāga or some other commentator who gave this meaning to the definition. Thus interpreted, it teaches the doctrine embodied in Diṅnāga's definition.

percept' is overlaid. Thus (on the *Bauddha* view) such a whole as a pot would not be an object of perception, so defined: *rūpādibhya utpannaṁ jñānaṁ ghaṭasya vyapadiśyate,—na tato bhaviṣyatīty apakṣiptam.* The knowledge which is designated as knowledge *of the jar* is knowledge arising from colours, etc.: and therefore it does not arise 'from just that thing of which it is designated as the knowledge.' Uddyotakara's retort is that the Bauddha theory that substances are nothing apart from qualities is baseless; and that the cognition arising from colour is in point of fact designated the knowledge *of colour*, and not the knowledge of a pot.

The other point of interest is Uddyotakara's concluding argument against the '*sūtra*,' as he calls the definition of Vasubandhu (*NV*, p. 43, l. 13). He says: *grāhya-grāhaka-jñānayor ayugapad-bhāvāj jñānaṁ apratyakṣaṁ syāt*—"the knowledge would be other than perception, because the reality apprehended and the apprehending cognition will not be simultaneous." Vācaspati Miśra explains that the *grāhya* is the thing from which the knowledge arises; and that it is the *cause* of which the knowledge is the *effect*. The knowledge cognises *as present* its own cause: but its cause—being, *quā* cause, the antecedent of the knowledge which is the effect—is, as such, *past*. The cognition therefore is false: and, being false, it cannot be perception. He then cites (*NVT*, p. 101, l. 14) a couplet: *yathā 'ha :*

> *bhinna-kālaṁ kathaṁ grāhyam iti ced, grāhyatāṁ viduḥ*
> *hetutvam eva, tad-yuktaṁ jñānākārārpaṇa-kṣamam.*

"If you ask how that which is separated in time can be the object grasped, the answer is that being an object just means being a cause (of the knowledge); and that which has this property (of being a cause of the knowledge) has the capacity of bringing about a presentation or idea (*jñānākāra*)." The answer given in this citation is paraphrased by Vācaspati: *bhinna-kālasyā 'pi sadṛśa-jñāna-jananam eva hi tasya taj-jñānaṁ prati grāhyatvaṁ, nānyat*—even if the object *is* separate in time (*i.e.* past), its production of a cognition like it and nothing else is what constitutes it the 'object' of that knowledge. Now this couplet is cited in the *Sarva-darśana-saṁgraha*[1] as embodying the *Sautrāntika* (realist) reply to a *Yogacāra* (idealist) criticism: and it is implied later on[2] that the doctrine of the *Vaibhāṣikas* corresponds to that of the *Sautrāntikas*, so that what is said of the one is in some respects applicable to the other. We know that Vasubandhu during a great part of his career was a follower of the *Vaibhāṣika* school, and adopted the *Yogācara* or *vijñāna-vāda* doctrine late in life under the influence of his brother Asaṅga. Is it not possible that he wrote his *Tarka-śāstra* as a *Vaibhāṣika?* If so, this couplet may well be his: as in fact seems to be the implication of the *yathā 'ha* with which Vācaspati here introduces it. This hypothesis would explain the persistent strain of realism in the Buddhist logic derived through Diṅnāga from Vasubandhu.

[Another citation made by Vācaspati in the present passage is merely a statement of a logical principle borrowed from the *Śloka-vārttika*. *yathā 'huḥ :—*

niyamas tad-virodhāc ca kalpyate, nāvirodhinaḥ.[3] "As has

[1] =Cowell and Gough, p. 28. My text, however, has *ca vyakter* in the second line, in place of *tadyuktam ;* and this reading is implied in Gough's translation.

[2] =Cowell and Gough, p. 33 *ad fin.* *SDS* represents both as realists: the difference being that the *Sautrāntika* held the real corresponding to presentation to be inferred, whereas the *Vaibhāṣika* denied that inference was possible in such a case, and maintained that things (objects, *artha*) are of two kinds, *grāhya* and *adhyavaseya.* The *SDS* then proceeds to explain *grāhya* by attributing to the *Vaibhāṣika* precisely that view of perception which we find in Diṅnāga—the idealist. And the distinction between the *grāhya* and the *adhyavaseya* is found in Dharmakīrti and Dharmottara, the logical heirs of Diṅnāga. It has been commonly recognised that Diṅnāga's logic is not really consistent with idealism. Is not the explanation perhaps that it was *not* an idealistic but a realistic logic that he inherited, and that he never succeeded in reconciling it with his own and his master's (later) idealism ?

[3] *Śl. Vārt., anumāna,* 55. But the Chaukhamba text reads *vipakṣāc ca,* with a variant *viruddhāc ca,* in place of *virodhāc ca.* Kumārila is defining the *pratijñā,* S is P, of an inference. This, he says, means that S is not non-P; it does not, however, preclude S from having other properties besides P, provided they do not contradict P.

been said, 'a universal statement is precluded from contradiction of what is predicated therein, and not from what does not contradict it.' "]

Section 5.—**Fragment B**: *Manas* as an Organ of Sense.

NA SUKHĀDI PRAMEYAṀ VĀ MANO VĀSTĪNDRIYĀNTARAM Fragment.
ANIṢEDHĀD UPĀTTAṀ CED ANYENDRIYA-RUTAṀ VṚTHĀ.

The two lines are separately cited by Vācaspati, but Vidyābhūṣaṇa identifies them with a passage in the first chapter of the *Pramāṇa-samuccaya* and cites them as forming one couplet. The meaning is: "Either pleasure, etc., are not *objects* of knowledge, or else *manas* must be an additional sense-organ." If you maintain (as Vātsyāyana does) that the *sūtra* accepts *manas* as a sense-organ on the ground that it does not deny this, then why does the *sūtra-kāra* put himself to the trouble of mentioning the other sense-organs? (the mention is useless, in virtue of the *tantra-yukti* of '*anumata*' to which Vātsyāyana appeals: for the other sense-organs, no less than *manas*, are mentioned in the sister-*śāstra*; and if the *sūtra-kāra* took *manas* for granted on this ground, he should also have taken the other sense-organs for granted). In the first line Diṅnāga is putting the dilemma which compels the *Vaiśeṣika* and the *Naiyāyika* to treat *manas* as a sense-organ. Both systems treat pleasure, pain, desire, cognition, etc., as qualities of the soul directly cognised, and as (like the qualities of other substances) *objects* of knowledge (*prameya*). If they are *prameya*, and perceptually cognised, it is necessary to invent an *indriya* for their perception, namely *manas*, as an organ of 'inner sense.'

Identification. Translation.

I take it that Diṅnāga's criticism here amounts to a charge of futility against the *sūtra-kāra*. The *sūtra-kāra* ought to have seen that he *must* make *manas* into an *indriya*, seeing that he has treated the psychical 'qualities' as *prameya*. But as a matter of fact the *sūtra-kāra* had not realised this plain consequence of his position. And Vātsyāyana, instead of deducing the *indriyatva* of *manas* from the *prameyatva* of *sukhādi* (as Praśastapāda deduced it from *Vaiśeṣika Sūtra*, V, ii, 15), falls back on this indefensible appeal to a *tantra-yukti* in order to import into his own system, *ab extra*, what is really implied in it already.

Source. The passages in the *NVT* in which these two lines are cited are:

NVT, p. 97, l. 1. *tad idam uktaṁ Diṅnāgena na sukhādi prameyaṁ vā mano vāstīndriyāntaram. na ca tat sambhavati, ghrāṇādi-sūtreṇa vibhāgapareṇa niṣedhād iti bhāvaḥ.*

That is: "This is Diṅnāga's point in the line 'either pleasure, etc., are not *prameya*, or else *manas* is another *indriya*.' But this is not possible (*i.e.* that *manas* should be an *indriya*), because it would contradict *NS*, I, i, 12, the object of which is to give an enumeration of the *indriya*'s (and this enumeration does not comprise *manas*)."

NVT, p. 97, l. 28. *tad dūṣitaṁ Diṅnāgena aniṣedhād upāttaṁ ced anyendriya-rutaṁ vṛthā.* '*tad*' here refers to *NBh*, p. 13, l. 9 (the appeal to the *tantra-yukti* of *anumata*. As a matter of fact, however, Vātsyāyana uses other arguments as well; but it must be admitted that he does not succeed in proving that the *sūtra-kāra* recognised *manas* as an *indriya*).

SECTION 6.—**Fragment C**: IS THE ORGAN IN CONTACT WITH THE OBJECT, IN VISION?

NVT, p. 76, l. 28. *yathoktam Diṅnāgena:*

Line 1. SĀNTARA-GRAHAṆAṀ NA SYĀT PRĀPTAU, JÑĀNE 'DHIKASYA CA,

bahir vartitvād indriyasyopapannam sāntara-grahaṇam iti ced, ata uktam:

Line 2. ADHIṢṬHĀNĀD BAHIR NĀKṢAM. . . .

kiṁtv adhiṣṭhāna-deśa evendriyam. kutaḥ?

. . . TAC-CIKITSĀDI-YOGATAḤ.

Line 3. SATYAPI CA BAHIR-BHĀVE NA ŚAKTI-VIṢAYE[1] KṢAṆE

Line 4. YADI CA SYĀT TADĀ PAŚYED APY UNMĪLYA NIMĪLANĀT

[1] Read *śaktir viṣaye*. See next note.

yadi ca syād, unmīlya nimīlita-nayano 'pi rūpaṁ paśyet. unmīlanād asti bahir indriyam iti.

The sense of these two couplets, when disentangled from the interspersed comment, is clear except for the second halves of lines 1 and 3. There is a long discussion dealing with this and cognate difficulties in the *Nyāya-vārttika* passage (pp. 35-38) on which Vācaspati is here commenting. Uddyotakara gives various reasons which have been brought to prove that the organs of sense, and in particular the visual organ, work without getting at the object (*aprāpya-kāritva*). One of these reasons is *sāntara-grahaṇāt*—the reason here adduced by Diṅnāga. Uddyotakara says this may either mean (*a*) 'because it grasps an object at a distance,' or (*b*) 'because it grasps the object with the intervening space.' Vācaspati cites Diṅnāga in connection with Uddyotakara's refutation of '*sāntara-grahaṇād aprāpya-kāritva*' in the latter sense. Another of the reasons mentioned by Uddyotakara as urged against the view that the visual organ acts through contact with its object is *pṛthutara-grahaṇāt*, 'because it apprehends things bigger than itself.' This seems to be the meaning of Diṅnāga's *jñāne 'dhikasya ca* in the first line of this fragment. But the remainder of Uddyotakara's discussion goes beyond what is urged in this fragment on the one hand; and on the other hand Uddyotakara does not deal with the objections raised in lines 2-4. Therefore Diṅnāga can hardly be the only, or even the principal, critic whom Uddyotakara has in view.

"There would not be apprehension of the object together with intervening space if the visual organ were in contact with its object; and, if there is apprehension of what exceeds (the eye in size), (such apprehension is not to be explained by a distinction between the 'visual organ' and the 'eye,' for) the 'visual organ' does not go forth from its place (the 'eye') —since it is to this (the definite part of the body called the eye) that medical treatment and so on is directed (on the assumption that the eye *is* the visual organ). And even if we Translation.

grant that the 'visual organ' might exist outside its bodily site 'the eye,' it would not have the power to act on the momentary existent which is its object.[1] And if it could, a man who had opened his eyes and then shut them would still see (when his eyes were shut)."

SECTION 7.—Fragment D: CRITICISM OF A POINT IN THE *Vaiśeṣika* ACCOUNT OF THE PERCEPTIBILITY OF SUBSTANCE.

Source. *NVT*, p. 129, l. 22. *na ca samuccīyamānāvadhāraṇaṁ Diṅnāgo mene, yad evam ūce vaiśeṣika-lakṣaṇa-dūṣaṇāvasare:*

Prose fragment. YADI RŪPAM EVA CĀKṢUṢAṀ TATO NA DRAVYAṀ CĀKṢUṢAṀ SYĀT TATHĀ CA MAHAD-ANEKA-DRAVYA-SAMAVAYĀD RUPĀC COPALABDHIR ITI DRAVYA-CĀKṢUṢATVĀBHIDHĀNAṀ VYĀHANYETA

—iti. atra hi pūrvavad dravya-sahita-rūpam eva cākṣuṣaṁ na gandha-rasādīti śakyaṁ samuccīyamānāvadhāraṇam.

That is: Diṅnāga did not hold the doctrine of aggregative restriction (which Dharmakīrti applies to the interpretation of the *trairūpya*), since he speaks thus when he is criticising the *Vaiśeṣika* definition (of perception):

Translation of fragment. "If colour *only* is the object of vision then substance cannot be an object of vision: and thus there would be contradiction of the assertion of the visibility of substance which is made in the words 'and perception arises from colour and from inherence in a substance which has magnitude and is composed of many parts.'"

Vācaspati explains that, as *tat-tulya eva* in the *trairūpya* has

[1] The text reads *bahir-bhāvena.* I have divided *bahir-bhāve na.* Further, I have rendered as if *saktir viṣaye.* I take the meaning to be that on the assumption that the 'visual beam' goes out to its object, it would never reach the object: for by the time it got there a new momentary existent would have taken the place of the original existent which the 'visual beam' went forth for to see. (This reverses the paradox which modern theories of vision—based on light coming *from* the object—carry with them. On the modern theory of vision what we see is always *past.* Diṅnāga's point on the contrary is that what we see is always *future.*)

been taken to mean 'only in the *sapakṣa* besides the *pakṣa*,' so here the *Vaiśeṣika* might have replied to Diṅnāga's criticism by saying that the *eva* conveys an 'aggregative restriction,' so that in saying 'only colour is visible' the meaning might be 'only colour *besides substance* is visible'—the intention being to exclude smell, taste, etc., from the sphere of visibility, and not substance.

Identification. The fragment being in prose cannot be from the *Pramāṇa-samuccaya* (unless Vācaspati is paraphrasing verse into prose). It might come from the *Pramāṇa-samuccaya-vṛtti*, a commentary attributed to Diṅnāga himself. Vidyābhūṣaṇa cites passages from the first chapter of the *Pramāṇa-samuccaya*, which quote not only *NS*, I, i, 4 with the *Bhāṣya* thereon, but also a *version* of *VS*, III, i, 18; and *VS*, V, ii, 15, in the form in which we have it, together with "the explanatory portion of the *Vaiśeṣika* definition"—the latter having some similarity to Praśastapāda's words. The citations embodied in the *Pramāṇa-samuccaya* are left unmetrical by Diṅnāga, apparently.

The citation made by Diṅnāga in the present passage is from the *Vaiśeṣika sūtra* (*mahad-aneka-dravya-samavayād rūpāc copalabdhiḥ*, *VS*, IV, i, 6). Cf. *PBh*, p. 186, l. 15. The three conditions which Praśastapāda there lays down for the perception of substance are apparently a true interpretation of the *sūtra*.

SECTION 8.—**Fragment E**: TESTIMONY IS NOT A SEPARATE SOURCE OF KNOWLEDGE.

Source. *NVT*, p. 138, l. 5. *atra śabdaṁ pramāṇāntaram asahamāno Diṅnāgas tal lakṣaṇaṁ vikalpya ākṣipati. āptopadesa iti. . . .*

Ibid., l. 19. *yathoktaṁ Bhadantena:*

Fragment. ĀPTA-VĀKYĀVISAṀVĀDA-SĀMĀNYĀD ANUMĀNATĀ

—iti.

Context. *NV*, p. 63, l. 13. *āptopadeśa iti kim āptānām avisaṁvādit-vaṁ vā pratipadyate, ahosvid arthasya tathā-bhāva iti. yady* *āptānāṁ avisaṁvaditvaṁ pratipadyate, tad anumānāt, arthasya tathā-bhāvaḥ, so 'pi pratyakṣeṇa. yadā hy ayam arthaṁ pratyakṣeṇopalabhate, tadā tathā-bhāvam arthasya pratipadyata iti.*

That is: Diṅnāga, not admitting testimony as a separate instrument of knowledge, attacks the definition (of *NS*, I, i. 7—*āptopadeśaḥ śabdaḥ*) by means of a dilemma which is stated in the *Vārttika* passage commencing *āptopadeśa* (*i.e.* the passage here cited).

The dilemma is: 'trustworthy authority' means either that the trustworthy *person* speaks truly, or else it means that the *thing* spoken is trustworthy and true. If it means the former—the credibility of the person—the belief is derived from inference. If it means the latter—the truth of the statement—this is a matter of perception: for it is when the person apprehends in perception the thing (about which the statement is made) that he realises the truth of the statement.

Diṅnāga in the present fragment is dealing with the former horn of the dilemma: which is that 'credible testimony' means the assertions of persons who are credible. He says that the belief in any particular statement then rests on an inference:

Translation. "The belief is inferential, the ground of it being the common character of corroboratedness belonging to the statements of the 'trustworthy' person."

Identification. This fragment is identified by Vidyābhūṣaṇa (*HIL*, p. 288, note 1) with a passage in the second chapter of the *Pramāṇa-samuccaya*.

SECTION 9.—**Fragment F**: WHAT IS THE 'PROBANDUM' ('*anumeya*') IN INFERENCE?

NVT, p. 120, l. 10. *atra Diṅnāgena dhūmād agni-rūpa-dharmāntarānumānam agnideśayoḥ saṁbandhānumānaṁ ca dūṣayitvā 'gni-viśiṣṭadeśānumānaṁ samarthitam. tathā cāha—*

Fragment.
Line 1. KECID DHARMĀNTARAṀ MEYAṀ LIṄGASYĀVYABHICĀRATAḤ.
Line 2. SAṀBANDHAṀ KECID ICCHANTI SIDDHATVĀD DHARMA-DHARMIṆOḤ.

LIṄGAṀ DHARME PRASIDDHAṀ CET KIM ANYAT TENA MĪYATE ? Line 3.
ATHA DHARMIṆI, TASYAIVA KIM-ARTHAṀ NĀNUMEYATĀ ? Line 4.
SAṀBANDHE 'PI DVAYAṀ NĀSTI, ṢAṢṬHĪ SRŪYETA TAD-VATI. Line 5.
AVĀCYO 'NUGṚHĪTATVĀN NA CĀSAU LIṄGA-SAṀGATAḤ. Line 6.

—*na hi saṁbandha-dharmatayā liṅgaṁ pramīyate, api tu deśa-saṁgatam ity arthaḥ.*

LIṄGASYĀVYABHICĀRAS TU DHARMEṆĀNYATRA DṚŚYATE Line 7.
TATRA PRASIDDHAṀ TAD-YUKTAṀ DHARMIṆAṀ GAMAYIṢYATI Line 8.

—*iti.*

That is: Diṅnāga criticises first the view that what we infer from smoke is another quality, viz. fire, and secondly the view that we infer the relation between fire and place; and he accepts the view that we infer the place qualified by fire. Thus he says: **Translation of fragment.**

" Some hold that another quality is the thing to be inferred from the invariability of the syllogistic mark (middle term). Line 1.

" Others will have it that the relation is inferred, on the ground that the quality (P, fire) and the subject (S, the hill) are already known (and therefore cannot be things to be inferred. Fire *as such* is not a thing to be inferred, nor is the hill *as such*). Line 2.

" If the syllogistic mark (M, smoke) has been given before in the quality (P, fire), what *different* thing is it that is said to be inferred through the mark ? (P must have been presented before, *ex hypothesi*, when we experienced the concomitance between M and P). Line 3.

" Or if it was experienced in the subjects or possessors of fire (such as the hearth), why is not just this (the fiery hearth, the fire *of the hearth*) that is inferred ?[1] Line 4.

[1] Fire *in general* cannot be the thing to be inferred, because fire in general is already known. And the fire of past experience, as *particularised* by residence in the hearth, etc., of course cannot be the *probandum*—we do not infer the fire of the hearth from the smoke on the hill. (*dharmin* commonly means S, the subject in which the property is to be inferred. But it also means in general a property-possessor, and so may apply to the *sapakṣa*, XP, as well as to the *pakṣa*, S.)

Line 5. "In the relation, on the other hand, there is not the double aspect (which marks the genuine *anumeya*).[1] And you would use the genitive case in referring to something possessing something else[2] (so that the Proposition to be proved should take the form *parvatasyāgnir asti*, there is hill's fire—instead of *parvate 'gnir asti*, there is fire on the hill).

Line 6. "The relation is not intended to be referred to by the speaker, since it is merely implicit in the statement.[3] And it is not the relation that is concomitant with the syllogistic mark (M, smoke).[4]

[1] Cf. *Śl. Vārt.*, *anumāna-pariccheda*, 32: *na cākāra-dvayaṁ tasya sādhya-sādhana-bhāg bhavet.* The *anumeya* is both *gamaka* and *gamya*, both M and—problematically—P. In other words it is the *ekadeśin* which has two *ekadeśas*, as *sādhana* and as *sādhya*. But the *relation* between hill and fire does not have fire as one aspect and smoke as another. It is the hill (of which fire is to be proved) that possesses both smoke and—problematically—fire.

[2] *Cf.* the commentators on Pāṇini, II, iii, 50, *ṣaṣṭhī śeṣe*. The sixth inflection, *i.e.* genitive, expresses mere relation, *e.g.* that between a thing and its possessor. It does not express a *kāraka*-function. The locative on the other hand does express a *kāraka*-function, viz. the *adhikaraṇa* of the action.

[3] Cf. *Śl. Vārt.*, *loc. cit.*: *tasmād artha-gṛhītatvān matub-arthasya gamyatā, na svātantryeṇa mantavyā.* What if the Proposition is put in the form *parvato vahnimān*, the hill is fire-possessing ? Does not the affix *-matup*, the possessive affix, express *mere* relation, as the genitive case-inflection does ? The reply given by Diṅnāga and by Kumārila seems to be that at any rate the relation, relegated to expression in a mere suffix, cannot claim the status of a 'term' in the inference.

[4] Cf. *Śl. Vārt.*, *loc. cit.*, 31: *na cāpy anugamas tena lingasyeha nidarśyate ;* and the comment: *udāharaṇe 'pi liṅgasya na saṁbandhenānugamaṁ darśayanti.* The major premise does not assert that where there is smoke there is *relation* (between hill and fire). The comment which Vācaspati Miśra inserts after line 6 takes a slightly different view of the meaning—"for the syllogistic mark is not apprehended as a property of the *relation :* it is connected with the *place*"—*i.e.* he takes the reference here to be to *pakṣa-dharmatā*, in the sense of residence of the middle term in the minor (and not in the major, as Pārthasārathi Miśra, the commentator on the *Śloka-vārttika* cited above, understands the parallel line in Kumārila's discussion). That is, we do not say that the *relation* is smoky: we say that the *hill* is smoky. As *anumeya* means indifferently S or P (really both together), either interpretation is possible.

"It is with the quality (P, fire) that the mark is seen, in other instances, to be concomitant. Line 7.

"And being found in those other cases it will prove the subject-as-connected-with-that-quality here (it will prove S-as-P)." Line 8.

This is the topic discussed in *Nyāyā-vārttika*, pp. 52-54, and *Śloka-vārttika*, *anumāna-pariccheda*, verses 23-34: both passages being closely parallel to the present fragment and written with Diṅnāga's discussion in view. In fact, some of the lines in this fragment are only intelligible in the light of what Kumārila says. **Parallel passages.**

Vidyābhūṣaṇa (*HIL*, p. 281) gives the Tibetan version of these eight lines as from *Pramāṇa-samuccaya*, Chapter II. **Identification.**

SECTION 10.—**Fragment G**: DEFINITION OF '*Anumāna*' OR THE INSTRUMENT OF INFERENTIAL KNOWLEDGE.

NV. p. 56, l. 14. *apare tu bruvate:*

NĀNTARĪYAKĀRTHA-DARŚANAṂ TAD-VIDO 'NUMĀNAM **Prose fragment.**

—*iti. asyārthaḥ: yo 'rtho yam artham antareṇa na bhavati, sa nāntarīyakaḥ: nāntarīyakas cāsāv arthaś ceti nāntarīyakārthaḥ: tasya darśanaṁ tav-vido 'numānam. yas tam veda. tan, nāntarīyako 'yam iti.*

That is:

Others, again, say:

"The experience of a thing which is inseparably connected with another thing is the instrument of inference for one who knows that it is inseparably connected." **Translation of fragment.**

The meaning is: a thing which does not exist without another thing is 'inseparably connected.' The compound *nāntarīyakārtha* is a *karma-dhāraya* compound, i.e. *nāntarīyaka* is in the position of adjective qualifying *artha*, and the compound as a whole is substantival. *Tad* in the compound *tad-vidaḥ* means 'that this is inseparably connected.' (Uddyotakara's criticism is to the effect that the *karma-dhāraya* compound is objectionable because the second member, 'thing,' is superfluous—since what is inseparably connected cannot but be a 'thing';[1] and that the addition 'for one who knows this' is also superfluous, since such knowledge is already implied in calling the thing *nāntarīyaka*.[2] The definition ought therefore to be reduced to: *nāntarīyaka-darśanam anumānam.*)

Identification of fragment.

Vidyābhūṣaṇa does not notice this fragment. But Vācaspati Miśra's statements at *NVT*, p. 127, l. 1 and l. 12 (see here next fragment, and fragment P) attribute the definition beyond possibility of doubt to Diṅnāga, and seem to imply clearly that it is given in a passage immediately preceding that in which the next fragment—*anumeye 'tha*, etc.—occurs: that is, in Chapter II of the *Pramāṇa-samuccaya*. But the present fragment is in prose, irreducible to *anuṣṭubh* metre. We must suppose either that there are unmetrical passages or phrases embodied in the *Pramāṇa-samuccaya*, or else that this comes from the *vṛtti*—which must then be in organic connection with the *Pramāṇa-samuccaya* itself, and not a commentary subsequently composed by Diṅnāga.

SECTION 11.—**Fragment H**: THE THREE CHARACTERS OF A VALID MIDDLE TERM.

NV, p. 58, l. 2. *apare tu manyante:*

Fragment (one line).

ANUMEYE 'THA TAT-TULYE SADBHĀVO NĀSTITĀ 'SATI

—*ity anumānam.*

That is: some again hold that the instrument of inference consists in:—

Translation of fragment.

"The presence of the middle term in the subject of the

[1] Keith, *ILA*, p. 104 *ad fin.* seems to have taken this to mean that a thing (on the *Bauddha* view) cannot but be inseparably connected.

[2] He adds by way of illustration: "For an inhabitant of *Nārikela-dvīpa*, on seeing smoke, does not think of it as '*nāntarīyaka*,' inseparably connected." Dr. Jhā (transl., vol. i, p. 188) adds the query—"where there is no fire?" and this would explain the illustration.

inference; its presence again in what is like the subject of the inference; and its absence in what is not (like the subject)."

NVT, p. 127, l. 12. *tad anena Diṅnāgasya lakṣaṇaṁ dūṣayitvā 'nyeṣāṁ lakṣaṇaṁ dūṣitam. saṁprati Diṅnāgasya svakīya-lakṣaṇa-prapañcārthaṁ vākyam anumeye 'tha tat-tulya ityādy upanyasya dūṣayati—apare tv iti.* **Identification of fragment.**

That is: by thus refuting the definition (of *anumāna*—see preceding fragment) given by Diṅnāga, he has refuted definitions given by others. Now he cites and refutes the formula—*anumeye 'tha tat-tulya*, etc.—which Diṅnāga gives in explanation of his definition.

Vidyābhūṣaṇa (*HIL*, p. 288, n. 2) gives the Tibetan version of this line as from Chapter II of the *Pramāṇa-samuccaya*. Vācaspati in the passage just cited states that it is an amplification or exposition of the definition of *anumāna* given in the preceding fragment—which may, therefore, also be assigned to Chapter II (perhaps of the *vṛtti*).

Bearings of the fragment. The importance of the fragment is indicated by the fact that Uddyotakara devotes a considerable passage (*NV*, pp. 58-59) to criticism of it. It is Diṅnāga's formula for the *trairūpya*, parallel to the couplet which occurs in Praśastapāda's *Bhāṣya*, p. 200, l. 19:

> *yad anumeyena saṁbaddhaṁ prasiddhaṁ ca tad-anvite*
> *tad-abhāve ca nāsty eva, tal liṅgam anumāpakam.*

The three notes of a '*nantarīyakārtha*' are presence in the *pakṣa*, presence in the *sapakṣa*, and absence in the *vipakṣa*. The formula belongs to a time when the doctrine of *vyāpti* had not yet developed. Diṅnāga combines it with that doctrine, and thereby exposes the formula to the criticism brought by Uddyotakara: a criticism which turns on the fact that *anumeya* is now taken in two senses at once—as S (minor) and as P (major).

Section 12.—(Note to Fragment H): A Septenary of Syllogisms.

In the passage which concludes Uddyotakara's criticism of this formula of the *trairūpya*, a doctrine of a septenary of possible types of syllogism is represented as following from the application of this formula. The context makes it plain that the doctrine is Diṅnāga's; but it is not clear how far it is stated in Diṅnāga's own words. Uddyotakara states the same doctrine a second time, in almost the same words, in another connection (*NV*, p. 131, l. 18).[1]

NV, p. 59, l. 11. *yad apy eka-dvi-pada-paryudāsena saptikā-saṁbhave ṣaṭ-pratiṣedham uktvā tri-lakṣaṇo hetur abhidhīyate, etad api . . . ayuktam.*

That is: there are seven possibilities, and he rejects six (as invalid middle terms) on the ground of failing to satisfy one or two of the three clauses of the *trairūpya*; the seventh (which satisfies all three clauses) is called 'the reason with three characteristics' (and is alone valid).

The seven possibilities are:

1. Resident in *pakṣa* (absent in *sapakṣa*, present in *vipakṣa*).
2. Resident in *sapakṣa* (absent in *pakṣa*, present in *vipakṣa*).
3. Absent in *vipakṣa* (absent in *pakṣa*, absent in *sapakṣa*).

The above three fail to satisfy *two* clauses.

4. Present in *pakṣa*, resident in *sapakṣa* (but not absent in *vipakṣa*).

5. Present in *pakṣa*, absent in *vipakṣa* (but not present in *sapakṣa*).

6. Present in *sapakṣa*, absent in *vipakṣa* (but not present in *pakṣa*).

These three fail to satisfy *one* clause. Uddyotakara maintains that, on the Buddhist's own showing, arguments which really come under head 4 are valid; and that arguments

[1] Dr. Jhā (transl., p. 371 footnote) reads into this passage a statement that this doctrine comes from a *Bauddha* '*vārttika*.' But Uddyotakara is plainly referring to his own *Vārttika* on I, i, 5.

under head 5 are valid, if there is no *sapakṣa*. Heads 4 and 5 are *kevalānvayin* and *kevala-vyatirekin*, in case there is no *vipakṣa* (in the former case) and no *sapakṣa* (in the latter case).

7. The *trilakṣaṇa-hetu* — present in *pakṣa*, present in *sapakṣa*, absent in *vipakṣa*.

It may be presumed that this doctrine is taught in the second chapter of the *Pramāṇa-samuccaya*. The scheme of seven types differs in principle from the scheme of nine types set out in fragment J, *q.v.*

SECTION 13.—VASUBANDHU AS A CRITIC OF THE *Nyāya*.

(Introductory to fragments from Chapters III and IV of the *Pramāṇa-samuccaya.*)

Chapter III deals with 'inference for another' (*parārthānumana*), which is the rubric corresponding to the *pañcāvayava-vākya*, the syllogism and its five members, in *Naiyāyika* works. Diṅnāga, like Praśastapāda, emphasises the distinction between inference *as such* and inference as *expressed in words*; and he criticises the definitions of the 'members' of the syllogism given in the *Nyāya Sūtra* on the ground that they fail to keep this distinction clear (see fragment L). But Diṅnāga was not the first Buddhist critic of these definitions. A writer, 'Subandhu,' who may reasonably be identified with Vasubandhu, criticises the definitions given in the *Nyāya Sūtra* of Proposition, Reason, and Exemplification (the first three 'members' of the syllogism), as is clear from the following passages of the *Vārttika* and *Tātparya-ṭīkā*:

NV, p. 139, l. 14. *tad etasmin avayava-traye evam lakṣaṇenopapādite teṣām trayo durvibhāvā ity anena vākyena mahānaiyāyikatvam ātmanaḥ khyāpitaṁ bhavati.*

NVT, p. 205, l. 26. *atra Subandhunā pratijñādayas trayo 'vayavā durvihitā Akṣapāda-lakṣaṇenety uktam: tad dūṣayati tad etasminn iti.*

That is: Uddyotakara says (ironically) that the writer who

states that three confused definitions of these members are given when Proposition, Reason, and Exemplification are thus defined, only shows by this statement what a great logician he himself is. Vācaspati adds that in this passage Uddyotakara is criticising the statement made by 'Subandhu,' to the effect that the three members—Proposition, etc.—are badly formulated by Akṣapāda's definitions.

Who was Subandhu? Dr. Jhā says: "It has been suggested that this name should be Vasubandhu, but the *Tātparya-ṭīkā* often speaks of '*saubandhavaṁ lakṣaṇam*,' which shows that there was a Buddhist logician Subandhu" (transl., vol. i, p. 394, on *NS*, I, i. 37). But there seems to be no other trace of this supposed 'Subandhu,' and the reasonable supposition is that in these passages Vācaspati abbreviates Vasubandhu to Subandhu:[1] just as he invariably speaks of Dharmakīrti as Kīrti. Vasubandhu's definition of perception is given at *NV*, p. 42, l. 15, and in that case Vācaspati (*NVT*, p. 99, l. 13) gives him the benefit of his full name—*Vāsubandhavaṁ pratyakṣa-lakṣaṇam.* A definition of *vāda* is given at *NV*, p. 151, l. 20, and here Vācaspati (*NVT*, p. 218, l. 9) calls it *saubandhavaṁ lakṣaṇam.* (Jhā's note here suggests that Subandhu may be Vasubaṇdhu, after all: and he thinks that 'Subandhu' must be the author of the *Vāda-vidhi* referred to by name at *NV*, p. 121, l. 2.—Jhā's transl., vol. i, p. 441 note.) A definition of *pratijñā*, Proposition, is given as from the *Vāda-vidhi* in the *NV* passage just referred to, viz. p. 121, l. 2. Whether 'Subandhu' is the author of this work, as he is stated by Vācaspati to be the author of the definition of *vāda* (*NV*, p. 151, and *NVT*, p. 218, above referred to), is not perfectly clear,[2] but seems highly probable.

[1] Similarly Vāmana, *Kāvyalāṅkāra-sūtra-vṛtti*, III, ii, 2, is quoted in Vidyābhūṣaṇa, *HIL*, p. 267, as having Subandhu for Vasubandhu.

[2] There is a doubt as to the reading at *NV*, p. 156, l. 17. Dr. Jhā reads the textual *vādābhidhānam* as *vāda-vidhānam*, which latter he takes as an alternative title of the work *Vāda-vidhi*. See his translation, vol. i, p. 454 footnote. The alternative title *vāda-vidhāna* only occurs at *NV*, p. 120, l. 6, in a reference to a *vāda-vidhāna-ṭīkā*, so far as I know.

Vidyābhūṣaṇa, on the authority of Sugiura, states that "when Hwen-Thsang was travelling in India he saw three works on the art of debate attributed to Vasubandhu. The Sanskrit originals of these works, as well as their Chinese versions, are now lost. The works were styled in Chinese: (1) *Ronki* (*vāda-vidhi*—the method of debate), (2) *Ronshiki* (*vāda-mārga*—the course of debate), and (3) *Ronshin* (*vāda-kauśala*—the expedients of debate" (*HIL*, p. 267). He also gives an account (*ibid.*) of a *Tarka-śāstra* attributed to Vasubandhu, of which a Chinese version exists: and in the first chapter of this Vasubandhu is said to deal with the five members of the syllogism, *pratijñā*, etc.

The evidence then is to the effect that Vācaspati's Subandhu is Vasubandhu, and that he is (perhaps) the author of the *Vāda-vidhi* quoted by Uddyotakara: and of definitions of perception, of *vāda*, and perhaps[1] of *pratijñā*, quoted and

[1] The definition of *pratijñā* given as from the *Vāda-vidhi* is *sādhyābhidhānam pratijñā* (*NV*, p. 121, l. 2). At *NV*, p. 161, l. 14, a definition of *pakṣa* is given—*pakṣo yaḥ sādhayitum iṣṭaḥ*—which Dr. Jhā, in a footnote to his translation, p. 331, says is "put forward by the *Bauddha* logician Subandhu." He does not say what authority he has for attributing this to 'Subandhu.' Vācaspati merely attributes it to a *Bauddha*—*Bhadantenānyathā lakṣaṇam praṇītam* (*NVT*, p. 184, l. 11). [Another definition is given of *pakṣa* at *NV*, p. 119, l. 4: *vicāraṇāyām iṣṭo 'rthaḥ pakṣaḥ*.]

The metrical definition of *pakṣa* which is given at *NV*, p. 119, ll. 15-16—*sādhyatvenepsitaḥ pakṣo viruddhārthānirākṛtaḥ*—is characterised by Vācaspati at *NVT*, p. 187, l. 14 as *sthānāntarīyaṁ Bhadantasya lakṣaṇam*. It is not clear who the Bauddha is to whom Vācaspati is referring; but it looks as if it were the same '*Bhadanta*' who gave the former definition, viz. *pakṣo yaḥ sādhayitum iṣṭaḥ*. The metrical definition looks like a fragment of Diṅnāga (*a*) because of the *anuṣṭubh* metre: (*b*) because the addition *viruddhārthānirākṛta* teaches the doctrine of *pakṣābhāsa* found in the *Nyāya-praveśa* ascribed to Diṅnāga, and the definition is in meaning identical with Praśastapāda's at *PBh*, p. 233, last line (and resemblance to Praśastapāda is a mark of Diṅnāga's writings); and (*c*) because, as Jhā points out (transl., p. 338 footnote), it also resembles Dharmakīrti's definition in the *Nyāyabindu: svarūpenaiva svayam-iṣṭo 'nirākṛtaḥ*. If it is from Diṅnāga it might come from the third chapter of the *Pramāṇa-samuccaya*. But Vidyābhūṣaṇa (*HIL*, p. 282, n. 2) cites as from that chapter two Tibetan lines, and says that "the Sanskrit original should run thus: *svarūpenaiva*

criticised by Uddyotakara. We may further conclude that Vasubandhu preceded Diṅnāga in his criticism of the definitions of Proposition, Reason, and Exemplification given in the *Nyāya-sūtra*.

SECTION 14. — **Fragment I**: (i) DEFINITION OF 'INFERENCE FOR ANOTHER' (*parārthānumāna*). (ii) A PROOF MUST BE ACCEPTED BY BOTH PARTIES.

Nyāya-ratnākara, p. 252 (commenting on *Śloka-vārttika*, *nirālambana-vāda*, verses 145-146): *bhavadīyenāpi*—

Fragment (i) (one line). PARĀRTHĀNUMĀNAṀ TU SVADṚṢṬĀRTHA-PRAKĀŚAKAM

iti lakṣaṇena sva-pratipannam eva prāśnikebhyaḥ pratipādanīyam.

That is: "It is something that a person has himself apprehended that is to be conveyed to questioners—even on your own definition:—

---

nirdeśyaḥ svayam-iṣṭaḥ svadharmiṇi pratyakṣārthānumānena cāpta-vācā 'nirākṛtaḥ."

At *NV*, p. 120, l. 2 *ff*. Uddyotakara attacks the introduction of the word *svayam* into a *Bauddha* definition. It looks at first as if the *svayam* criticised were part of the second or metrical definition above—for Uddyotakara says *svayaṁ sādhyatvenepsita iti*. (With this addition the definition comes close to the *Nyāyabindu* definition, and also to Vidyābhūṣaṇa's reconstruction of the two lines from the *Pramāṇa-samuccaya*. Perhaps after all this line *is* the original of one of those two lines ?) At p. 120, l. 7, however, we are told that the author of the *Vāda-vidhāna-ṭīkā* defends the addition of *svayam* to the definition. The definition cited at *NV*, p. 116, l. 14 is quoted as *pakso yaḥ sādhayitum iṣṭaḥ*—without *svayam*. And yet it is apparently with reference to this phrase *sādhayitum iṣṭaḥ* that Uddyotakara criticises the defence of the use of *svayam* : for he makes a special point of the use here of the infinitive, *sādhayitum*. But then again the infinitive may perhaps be considered to be *implied* in the phrase *sādhyatvenepsitaḥ*. I must admit that I cannot see any further into this haze. But it looks as if Uddyotakara regarded the two definitions as for purposes of criticism two versions of one and the same view: the former erring by saying too little, and the latter by saying too much (*NV*, p. 120,.l. 1). I think that Vācaspati meant to attribute them both to one person; and on the whole I incline to the view that Diṅnāga was this person (this latter opinion being partly derived from an impression—not easy to justify—that Vācaspati uses 'Bhadanta' specifically of Diṅnāga).

'Inference for another sets forth an object which has been apprehended by oneself.'" **Translation of fragment.**

Pārthasārathi Miśra is referring in *bhavadīya* to Diṅnāga, whom he mentions by name more than once in the context. On p. 250 (commenting on verse 131, *loc. cit.*) he has said: *bhavadvṛddhair eva hi Diṅnāgācāryair* YO VĀDI-PRATIVĀDI-NIŚCITO HETUḤ SA SĀDHANAM *ity uktam.* That is: "Your own authority, the doctor Diṅnāga, has said: 'A proof is a reason accepted by both parties to the discussion.'" And at p. 257 he again cites Diṅnāga by name (see fragment P below). Kumārila is arguing in this section of the *nirālambana-vāda* (which is probably directed largely against arguments urged by Diṅnāga in the *Ālambana-parīkṣā*) that the *Bauddha*—whose scepticism extends to reasoning itself—is inconsistent in using reasoning to confute his opponents. The *Bauddha* is represented as replying that so long as his opponent believes in reasoning it does not matter whether he (the *Bauddha*) himself believes in it or not: his arguments will still serve their purpose of convincing the opponent. Kumārila replies that this is inconsistent with the *Bauddha's* own statement about a means of proof—that both sides must admit it—and with his own definition of 'syllogism.' **Context.** **Fragment (ii) (prose).**

Diṅnāga's definition of *parārthānumāna* appears to be identical in meaning with that given by Praśastapāda (*PBh*, p. 231).

Vidyābhūṣaṇa (*HIL*, p. 282 footnote) draws attention to this fragment, and cites the Tibetan version as from *Pramāṇa-samuccaya*, Chapter III. **Identification of fragment (i).**

SECTION 15.—Fragment J: THE NINE REASONS OR TYPES OF ARGUMENT, VALID AND INVALID.

NVT, p. 197, last line *ff*. *atra Diṅnāgena:* **Fragment (8 lines).**

SAPAKṢE SANN ASAN DVEDHĀ PAKṢA-DHARMAḤ PUNAS TRIDHĀ **Line 1.**
PRATYEKAM ASAPAKṢE CA SAD ASAD DVIVIDHATVATAḤ **Line 2.**

iti. na ca pakṣa-dharmān hetu-tad-ābhāsān darśayitvā,

Line 3. TATRA YAḤ SAN SAJATĪYE DVEDHĀ CĀSAṀS TAD-ATYAYE
Line 4. SA HETUR, VIPARĪTO 'SMĀD VIRUDDHO 'NYAS TV ANIŚCITAḤ.

iti hetu-tad-ābhāsa-viveko darśitaḥ. tasyārthaḥ, yaḥ pakṣa-dharmaḥ sa sapakṣe sann asan dvedhā iti. sa punar asapakṣe sad asad dvividhatvataḥ. pratyekaṁ tridhā bhavatīti. pakṣa-dharmaḥ sapakṣe san vipakṣe sad asad dvividhatvatas tridhā. pakṣa-dharmaḥ sapakṣe dvedha vipakṣe sad asad dvividhatvatas tridheti. atrodāharaṇam:

Line 5. PRAMEYA-KṚTAKĀNITYA-KṚTA-ŚRĀVAṆA-YATNAJĀḤ
Line 6. ANITYA-YATNAJĀSPARŚĀ NITYATVĀDIṢU TE NAVA

nityatvādiṣu sādhyeṣu prameyatvādayo nava hetu-tad-ābhāsāḥ. teṣāṁ yathā-saṁkhyaṁ nityatvāditi. sādhyāny udāharanti—

Line 7. NITYĀNITYA-PRAYATNOTTHA-MADHYAMA-TRIKA-ŚĀSVATĀḤ
Line 8. AYATNĀNITYA-NITYĀŚ CA PRAMEYATVĀDI-SĀDHANĀḤ.

Translation. " Diṅnāga says:

Line 1. ' A middle term or quality of the subject of inference[1] first takes three forms, according as it does or does not reside in the two possible ways in the *sapakṣa*.[2]

[1] *pakṣa-dharma* is a general term which covers both *hetu* and *hetvābhāsa*, valid and invalid reasons. Vidyābhūṣaṇa (*HIL*, p. 299, n. 2) says—I do not know on what authority—that " the *hetu-cakra* is also called in Sanskrit *pakṣa-dharma-cakra*." The latter name is preferable, inasmuch as hetu commonly means a *valid* reason.

This treatment assumes that the *hetu* or *hevābhāsa is* a quality of the subject, i.e. *is pakṣa-dharma*. It therefore ignores the *asiddha-hetvābhāsa*, the pretended reason or middle term (M) which in fact does *not* reside in the subject (S). See fragment K. Thus it differs from the ' septenary of arguments ' (see Note to fragment H), because the septenary takes the *asiddha* into account.

[2] The two ways in which M does or does not reside in *sapakṣas*, XP's, are, first, residence or non-residence in *some* (not all); and secondly, esidence or non-residence in *all*. This gives a *threefold* relation of M to XP, viz.:

(i) Residence in *all sapakṣas*. All XP is M.

(ii) Residence in *some sapakṣas* (=non-residence in some). Some XP is M.

(iii) *Non*-residence in *all*. No XP is M.

'And in each of these three possible cases the middle Line 2.
term does or does not reside in the two ways in the
vipakṣa.'[1]

"So far he has not shown what middle terms are valid reasons and what are fallacious:

'Among these, a middle term which is present in (either Line 3.
of) the two ways[2] in the *sapakṣa*, and is absent in the *vipakṣa*, Line 4.
is a valid reason. What differs from this is either contradictory[3] or inconclusive.'[4]

[1] There is similarly a threefold division of possible relations of the middle term to the *vipakṣa*, X non-P, according as M is resident in *all* X non-P's, resident in *some* (non-resident in some), or *non*-resident in *all* (*i.e.* not resident in any X non-P).

Combining this threefold relation to the *vipakṣa* with the threefold relation to the *sapakṣa* we get the *nine* types of the '*hetu-cakra*':

I. All SP is M, all XP is M, all X non-P is M (inconclusive).
II. All SP is M, all XP is M, no X non-P is M (valid).
III. All SP is M, all XP is M, some X non-P is M (inconclusive).
IV. All SP is M, no XP is M, all X non-P is M (contradictory).
V. All SP is M, no XP is M, no X non-P is M (inconclusive).
VI. All SP is M, no XP is M, some X non-P is M (contradictory).
VII. All SP is M, some XP is M, all X non-P is M (inconclusive).
VIII. All SP is M, some XP is M, no X non-P is M (valid).
IX. All SP is M, some XP is M, some X non-P is M (inconclusive).

(These are arranged in the numerical order of the diagram facing p. 298 of Vidyābhūṣaṇa's *History of Indian Logic*, and p. 100 of his *Mediæval Logic*. They are there arranged in a square:

I.	II.	III.
IV.	V.	VI.
VII.	VIII.	IX.)

Dr. F. W. Thomas informs me that the Tibetan text shows the square arrangement.

[2] Either present in all *sapakṣas* or present in some only. *anvayinaḥ sapakṣa-vyāpty-avyāptibhyāṁ dvitvam*, as Uddyotakara says. There are thus two valid types, Nos. II and VIII of the list. As we should put it, BARBARA may be of two kinds according as the major premise is or is not simply convertible. (The middle must of course be absent in *all vipakṣas*, otherwise we should have an instance X non-P M, which would invalidate the *vyāpti* or 'major premise,' all M is P.)

[3] Nos. IV and VI are 'contradictory,' as leading in the valid types II and VIII to the contradictory conclusion.

[4] Nos. I, III, V, VII, IX—the odd numbers, or corners and centre of the square—are classed by Diṅnāga as *aniścita*=*saṁdigdha:* as

"In these lines the distinction between the reason or valid middle, and the apparent reason or invalid middle, is shown. The meaning of the first two lines is that a middle term, which is a quality of the minor, may be resident or non-resident in the *sapakṣa* in two ways; and again resident or non-resident in the *vipakṣa* in two ways: and in each case there is a threefold division. Being a quality of the minor, and being resident in the *sapakṣa*, it may be resident in two ways (in some or all), and non-resident in two ways (in some or all), in the *vipakṣa*, which means that there are three ways in which it may be related to the *vipakṣa* (as residing in all, some, or none). And then again, being a quality of the *pakṣa*, and being related in two (*further*)[1] ways to the *sapakṣa*, it may be resident and non-resident in the two ways in the *vipakṣa*—that is, related in three ways to the *vipakṣa*. He now gives the illustration:

Lines 5 and 6. 'The nine middle terms used to prove eternality and the other majors are: knowable, product, non-eternal; product, audible, effect of volition; non-eternal, effect of volition, intangible.'

"Knowable, etc., are the nine reasons and apparent reasons used to prove eternality and the other majors. Eternality, etc. belong to these in the order as enumerated. The following are the examples of the majors:

Lines 7 and 8. 'The majors which have knowable and so on for their middle terms are: eternal, non-eternal, effect of volition;

---

leading to a doubtful conclusion. The centre, No. V, is the *asādhāraṇa* of other logicians—the too restricted reason: which Praśastapāda classes as *anadhyavasita*—*i.e.* leading to no conclusion at all, not even to a doubtful one. The first type, No. I, is its opposite, the too general reason.

[1] Vācaspati's explanation of the way in which the nine types is arrived at is, I think, that given in footnotes 2 on p. 30 and 1 on p. 31, above; but instead of giving the second two sets of three separately he indicates them by the rather confusing phrase '*sapakṣe dvedhā.*' And the first set of three is indicated through the ambiguous *sapakse san*—which must be taken to mean 'resident in *all* the sapakṣas.' The punctuation of the text is wrong, and I have altered it.

in the middle set of three,[1] eternal; and non-volitional, non-eternal, eternal.' "

Vidyābhūṣaṇa (*HIL*, pp. 283-285 footnotes) cites the Tibetan version of this passage as from Chapter III of the *Pramāṇa-samuccaya*. Identification.

Uddyotakara, in commenting on *NS*, I, i, 35, returns to the subject of the *trilakṣaṇa-hetu* (already dealt with in his comment on I, i, 5). He repeats his argument against the *trairūpya*[2] (see fragment H) and against the ' septenary ' of types of argument (see Note to fragment H); and then he quotes the third line of the present fragment: *tatra yaḥ san sajātīye*, etc. (*NV*, p. 132, l. 12). He argues that this, as a definition of *hetu*, fails to mention the requirement of *pakṣa-dharmatā* as it stands. The *Bauddha* is then represented as replying that this deficiency is supplied in the next fragment, *q.v.* Context.

[1] The *madhyama-trika* is the middle line of the square, Nos. IV, V, and VI. Putting the middle terms of lines 5 and 6 together with the majors of lines 7 and 8 we get:

I. Sound is eternal because knowable.
II. Sound is non-eternal because a product.
III. Sound is volitional because non-eternal.
IV. Sound is eternal because a product.
V. Sound is eternal because audible.
VI. Sound is eternal because volitional.
VII. Sound is non-volitional because non-eternal.
VIII. Sound is non-eternal because volitional.
IX.. Sound is eternal because intangible.

These are exactly the examples given in the *Hetu-cakra-ḍamaru* (*i.e.* the *Nyāya-praveśa*): with this exception, that Vidyābhūṣaṇa gives non-eternal (instead of eternal) as the major of No. V.

[2] The discussion arises out of his citation and criticism of yet another *Bauddha* definition of the *hetu*, viz. *vipakṣād viśeṣaḥ* (*NV*, p. 128, l. 9 *ff.*). There is nothing to show the source of this citation except the fact that at p. 131, l. 10, Uddyotakara considers it from the standpoint of the *Sautrāntika* view that all things are non-eternal (*yadā Sautrāntika-pakṣam āśritya lakṣaṇaṁ vicāryate*, etc.).

SECTION 16.—**Fragment K**: ALL MIDDLE TERMS ARE '*Pakṣa-dharma.*'

NVT, p. 198, l. 14 *uktam Diṅnāgena*—

Fragment (one line).

SĀDHYA-DHARMO YATO HETUS TAD-ĀBHĀSAŚ CA BHŪYASĀ *iti.*

That is: Diṅnāga says:

Translation of fragment.

"Because the valid reason and the apparent reason are, in general, qualities of the Subject of the inference . . ."

Identification.

Vidyābhūṣaṇa does not notice this fragment. The sense of it is incomplete, and the *yataḥ* would appear to point to a correlative *tataḥ* in a following line. Diṅnāga may perhaps have said: "It is because both valid and spurious reasons are in general resident in S that this wheel of reasons does not concern itself with the relation of M to S." For, as Vidyābhūṣaṇa points out (*HIL*, p. 299), "in this work" (*i.e.* the *Hetu-cakra-ḍamaru*) "Diṅnāga has analysed all nine possible relations between the middle and the major terms," ignoring the relation between the middle and the minor as such. It seems probable that this may be a ninth line continuous with the eight lines of the preceding fragment. It is cited immediately in the context.

Context.

See preceding fragment. The *Bauddha*, in reply to criticisms, is represented by Uddyotakara as saying that the present fragment implies that a valid reason must be *pakṣa-dharma*, resident in SP.

NV, p. 132, l. 14. *yadi tāvad etal lakṣaṇam yathā-śruti bhavati, pakṣe*[1] *vidyata iti kenaital labhyate?—iti.*[2] *nanu coktaṁ hetuḥ tad-ābhāso vā prāyaḥ pakṣa-dharma eva bhavati.*

[1] The text reads *vipakṣe vidyate,* which cannot possibly be right. Dr. Jhā translates as if *pakṣe vidyate :* and this must be the true reading.

[2] The *iti* means that he is explaining his last sentence *etāvatā kila lakṣaṇena tri-lakṣaṇo hetur labhyata iti yathā-śruti na labhyate.* i.e., he is explaining the statement that the definition does *not*, as it stands, cover the *three* characters of the valid reason—because it omits the first character, *pakṣa-dharmatā.*

That is: if that definition (line 3 of preceding fragment) is taken as it stands, by what phrase does it say that the middle term resides in the *pakṣa*, SP ? (That is, it does *not* say so.) It may be suggested that it is also said, 'a reason, valid or invalid, is in general resident in SP.' (This paraphrases the line cited by Vācaspati.)

Uddyotakara says that the statement no doubt implies that M resides in SP; but it does not imply that M resides in *all* cases of SP: *satyam, arthāt pakṣa-dharmo gamyate: na tu vyāpake niyato labhyate*[1] (*NV*, p. 132, l. 20). It asserts *mere* concomitance, which may be either residence in *all* or in *some* (of S): *sambhava-mātraṁ labhyate, tac ca dvedhā, vyāpakam avyāpakaṁ ca.* The *Bauddha* falls back on his usual device of reading a restriction (*avadhāraṇa*) into the statement: *pakṣa-dharma* means *pakṣa-dharma and nothing else*, and the M which does not reside in all S cannot be called *pakṣa-dharma and nothing else*, because it resides only in part of S (*na tv ayam pakṣa-dharma eva, ekadeśa-vṛttitvāt*).[2] That which resides only in part of S cannot be called *pakṣasya dharma eva*. Uddyotakara replies that the restriction would not have the force of excluding a property resident only in some S (*katham avyāpakaṁ nivartayiṣyati ?*). It has a different force in Diṅnāga's statement (*anyārtham avadhāraṇaṁ kalpayanti bhavantaḥ*): *i.e.*, the force of 'distributing' the subject of the statement, viz. 'reasons and apparent reasons' (*hetu-*

[1] Jhā transl., vol. i, p. 374, renders "there is nothing to imply that *every* Probans *must* subsist in the Subject"—*i.e.* he understands the criticism to be that the statement does not imply that all M is P. But the context seems to me to make it plain that Uddyotakara means 'the statement does not imply that all SP is M.' His objection is that it would admit arguments with an illicit process of the minor term. *na vyāpake niyataḥ*, literally, means that the *pakṣa-dharma-hetu* is not confined to the case of a *pakṣa-dharma* which is *vyāpaka* of (belongs to *all* of) the *pakṣa*, S. (The interpretation of the rest of the passage which I give here differs accordingly from Dr. Jhā's rendering on p. 374.)

[2] To say that nothing but a property of S is M means that every M is a property of S: but it does not mean that all S is M, as the *Bauddha* here supposes.

tad-ābhāsa-niyama-jñāpanārtham): so that the statement would mean that "all reasons and apparent reasons are qualities of the subject of inference."[1]

SECTION 17.—**Fragment L**: DIṄNĀGA'S CRITICISM OF THE DEFINITION OF '*Hetu*,' I.E. OF THE SECOND MEMBER OF THE SYLLOGISM.

(*NS*, I, i, 34. *udāharaṇā-sādharmyāt sādhya-sādhanaṁ hetuḥ.*)

UDĀHARAṆA-SĀDHARMYĀT KIM ANYAT SĀDHYA-SĀDHANAM ?
SĀDHANAṀ YADI SĀDHARMYAM, NA VĀKYĀṀŚAḤ, NA PAÑCAMĪ.
. . . SĀDHANATVĀD ASAṀBHAVAḤ
. . . PRAKṚTE TV ANYA-SAṀBHAVAḤ
SVALAKṢAṆENA BĀDHĀ CEN, NA, VIKALPĀDI SAṀBHAVĀT.
TASMĀT ṢAṢṬHY ASTU, TATRĀPI VIŚEṢAṆAM ANARTHAKAM.

Actual citation seems to be confined to these four whole lines and two half-lines. The first is cited at *NV*, p. 123, l. 8, the rest at *NVT*, pp. 189, l. 16–190, l. 2. The latter passage, which I give *in extenso* below, gives what is either a paraphrase or an exposition of Diṅnāga's criticism, and it is not easy to disentangle actual citations in it.

The fragment was not noticed by Vidyābhūṣaṇa, although Dr. Jhā had drawn attention to it in a footnote to vol. i, p. 348 of his translation of the *Nyāya-bhāṣya* and *Vārttika*: "It is interesting to note that the *Tātparya* actually quotes fifteen[2] lines from the works of Diṅnāga embodying the objection here taken up by the *Vārttika*" (*i.e.* the objection *udāharaṇa-sādharmyāc ca kim anyat sādhya-sādhanam ity eke*—*NV*, p. 123, l. 8). "It is not possible, however, to translate this passage, as the text appears to be defective." The lines cited are attributed to Diṅnāga by name in *NVT*, p. 190, l. 2. They

[1] The remainder of the passage merely reiterates the arguments against the *trairūpya* already urged in the comment on I, i, 5.

[2] As just stated, I cannot find more than the fragment given above: but Vācaspati's paraphrase or exposition seems to imply a passage of eight or ten lines.

are probably to be found near the beginning of Chapter IV of the *Pramāṇa-samuccaya—i.e.*, the chapter of that work which, according to Vidyābhūṣaṇa (*HIL*, pp. 276 and 286), treats of Reason and Example.

The *Vārttika*'s account of the controversy.

Uddyotakara's reply to Diṅnāga's criticism is given in a rather lengthy and difficult section (*NV*, pp. 123, l. 8–125, l. 4) of his comment on *NS*, I, i, 34, which I render as follows:

" Some say that 'the means of proving the conclusion is not anything distinct from the likeness to the example,' and so the definition should be *svata udāharaṇa-sādharmyaṁ hetuḥ*—the reason (M) is the likeness of the thing itself (S) to the example (XP). And if you say that the words *sādhya-sādhanam*, instrument of proving the conclusion, are inserted as a qualification of *udāharaṇa-sādharmyam*, then the employment of the fifth or ablative case-inflection (in *udāharaṇa-sādharmyāt*) serves no purpose. We do not say *nīlād utpalam*, but *nīlam utpalam*, blue lotus (blue qualifies lotus, and has the same case-inflection therefore). Others[1] give a different account of the uselessness of the employment of the ablative, saying that the ablative is used in the case of two *different* things—as 'he comes from the village'; but 'the instrument of proof' is not something separate from the 'likeness to the example'; and therefore we cannot say 'the means of proof is *from* likeness to the example.' And if the *sūtra-kāra* means that 'likeness to the example, qualified[2] by being the means of proving what is to be proved,' is the *hetu*, or second 'member' of the syllogism or *pañcāvayava-vākya*, this amounts to saying that the *hetu*, as the second member of the syllogism, is (not a statement, *abhidhāna*, but) a thing stated

[1] It is not clear who these 'others' are, nor does their view appear to differ materially from the view just stated; which, according to Vācaspati, is what Diṅnāga meant by his '*na pancamī*'—*tad idam uktaṁ Bhadantena. anye tv etad anyathā vyācakṣate* (*NVT*, p. 190, l. 5).

[2] The qualification is necessary, as Uddyotakara points out below, because mere likeness to the example might be an irrelevant likeness, in which case, of course, it would not be the *hetu*. See *NV*, p. 123, last line to p. 124, *sādharmyasya vyabhicāry-avyabhichāritvād viśeṣaṇa-yogaḥ*.

(*abhidheya*).[1] And this would be inconsistent with the definition which has been given of the first member of the syllogism, the Proposition, which is defined as the *statement* of what is to be proved (*sādhya-nirdeśaḥ pratijñā*, *NS*, I, i, 33). A whole or aggregate made up of statements and things does not come within the range of possible experiences (*na cābhidhānābhidheyātmakaḥ samudāyo dṛṣṭaḥ*). Therefore both of these—the Proposition, as defined by the *Nyāya-sūtra*, and the Reason, as defined by the *Nyāya-sutra* on the present interpretation—*cannot* be 'members' of a single whole (*i.e.* they cannot both be members of the *pañcāvayava-vākya*).

"But this fault is not really chargeable against the *sūtra* (for the *sutra-kāra* really means, as interpreted by Vātsyāyana, that the *hetu* is the *statement* of the likeness to the example as probative of the *probandum*); and so Vātsyāyana makes no further answer to objections, because the only possible objection has been met by just this interpretation (*na parihārāntaraṁ prayojayati, tenaivāpākṛtatvāt*).

"It is said that a qualification is inserted (viz. the phrase *sādhya-sādhanam*) because the 'likeness' might be either conclusive or inconclusive (*sādharmyasya vyabhicāry-avyabhicāritvād viśeṣaṇa-yogaḥ*). The *Bauddha* objects that this is impossible on the ground that the *statement* of this (*i.e.* of *sādharmya*) does not admit of having this qualification (viz. probativeness) predicated of it (you could call the *likeness* to XP 'proof' that S is P; but you cannot call the *statement* of such likeness 'proof'). The nature of the subject is determined by the predicate (*yat tatprakāravat, tad viśeṣyate*); and the predicate or *prakāra* in this case, viz. 'probativeness,' belongs to the *likeness*, and not to the *statement* of the likeness (*sādharmye caitad asti, na ca vacasīti*).

[1] This is a fair criticism of the expressions used in the *sūtras*, which do as a matter of fact fail to make consistently explicit the distinction between inference and the verbal expression of inference—a distinction which *Vaiśeṣika-Bauddha* logic underlined through separate treatment of *svārthānumāna* and *parārthānumāna*.

"The *Naiyāyika's* reply to this is: We do not understand your position that 'the statement cannot have the predicate' (*vacasaḥ prakārakatvam*[1] *na bhavatīti na buddhyāmahe*). A word takes a qualification in precisely the same way in which a thing does (*yathaivārthaḥ prakāravān, tathā vacanam apīti*).[2] How *does* a thing get a predicate? From being either of two possibilities —*i.e.* because it is either of two—either eternal or non-eternal, either corporeal or incorporeal. Well, the word or statement also is either of two possibilities, and so the case is parallel: for the thing is named by the word—'eternal,' 'non-eternal'; 'corporeal,' 'incorporeal.' And we find that distinctions are in fact made between words as such. For instance, we are asked, 'What did he say?' and we answer, 'He said "*cow*"' (*gaur ity āha*). The *iti*, or the inverted commas, mark it as a *word:* and the word, as such, is distinguished from all other words. Moreover, the critic himself has used many sentences which make *distinctions* between different statements as such (*svayaṁ vacana-viśeṣakaṇi bahūni vākyāni prayuktāni*). For instance, he has defined Discussion (*vāda*) as 'statement with a view to proving and disproving one's own and the other party's position' (see fragment P). Here the critic, who has such a sharp sight for defects alleged in

[1] The text has *kārakatvam.* Dr. Jhā's emendation *prakārakatvam* seems highly probable.

[2] What Uddyotakara seems to me to be saying here is that there is necessarily parallelism between language and facts. If a fact is a proof, then a *statement* of the fact is a *probative* statement. And against Diṅnāga's denial of this latter corollary he has a most effective retort to hand in the former's definition of discussion as a *probative* statement! But he seems to prefer to deal with the matter as one of general principle rather than of particular application: so that he throws even this retort into the less obvious form of saying that in this definition Diṅnāga is attaching a predicate to a statement as such. Now to attach a predicate is to *distinguish.* And the fact is that we do distinguish one word from another, one statement from another. If then we ask further *how* one word is distinguished from another, we shall find the answer to be that distinctions between words are in virtue of, and exactly parallel to, the distinctions between the things or facts of which the words are the names. So that the name of the word is the name of the thing put within inverted commas.

others, has lost repute thereby" (read *sūkṣmekṣikayā* for *sūkṣmokṣikayā* of the text. Cf. *NVT*, p. 225, l. 2).

"As for the statement that the use of the ablative, *udāharaṇa-sādharmyāt—from* likeness to the example—is meaningless because we find the ablative used of a thing which is different from that which is asserted to be derived 'from' it (*arthāntare dṛṣṭatvāt*), in this he goes against his own school's teachings. For you *Bauddhas* do not believe that such wholes as 'army,' 'forest,' are anything *different* from their component parts—and yet the ablative is used in such sentences as 'this tree has been brought *from* the forest,' 'the horse comes *from* the army.' And (it may be added that) the ablative *is* found employed, in another branch of learning (the *arthaśāstra*), in application to things which are *not* different from the thing which is asserted to be derived 'from' them: for instance, it is said that 'the Six Virtues of a government are derived *from* making peace and waging war' (although making peace and waging war are enumerated *among* the Six Virtues).[1]

"Moreover, the definition of the valid reason as 'what differentiates from non-P'[2] is (intended by its *Bauddha* author to

[1] Presumably the use of the ablative here is to be defended on the ground that these two are basic, the other four derivative. It does not really affect the soundness of the principle laid down for the employment of the ablative. Nor does Uddyotakara seem to question that principle in general. He only suggests that it admits of qualification in a particular application.

[2] *hetur vipakṣād viśeṣaḥ*. Who was the particular *Bauddha* who gave this definition? Uddyotakara *need* not be taken to imply that it was Diṅnāga himself, though that is a natural supposition. He criticises this definition at length in his comment on the following *sūtra*, *NS*, I, i, 35 (*NV*, p. 128, l. 9 *ff.*). Vācaspati Miśra says nothing as to its authorship in his comment on either passage: but he may have meant us to take the attribution to Diṅnāga for granted, in view of the context. At *NV*, p. 129, l. 14, Uddyotakara refers to a commentary—*Vṛtti*—which he tells us qualifies the definition by adding the phrase *yo dharmaḥ pakṣasya*. It is possible, even probable, that the *vṛtti* here referred to is Diṅnāga's own *vṛtti* on his *Pramāṇa-samuccaya*, and that he is here supplementing his own definition as given in the *Pramāṇa-samuccaya*.

apply even in the case) of a *hetu* where a *vipakṣa*, or case of non-P, is not admitted to exist (as, for instance, in the argument 'sound is non-eternal, because it is a product.' According to the *Bauddha* tenet there is nothing eternal. Therefore the reason, 'being a product,' here differentiates the Subject, 'sound as non-eternal,' from a non-P which *does not exist*).[1] How then can you say that the ablative refers to *arthāntara*, a separate or different thing? (What does not exist cannot be called a separate thing, *arthāntara*.)

"As to the suggestion that the genitive case *udāharaṇa-sādharmyasya* would be more correct than the ablative *udāharaṇa-sādharmyāt*, this too is wrong: for the use of a *kāraka*-inflection (such as the ablative is—the genitive is not reckoned as a *kāraka*) depends on what the speaker means to say. When the likeness is intended to be referred to as the thing that is stated. ('the Reason is the statement of the probativeness *of* the likeness to the example'), the genitive case would be right. But when the likeness is intended to be spoken of as the cause of the statement, then the casual ablative is correct. You may ask: How is the likeness to the example the *cause* of the statement of the probativeness? The answer is that when such likeness is present the statement is made ('presence in presence,' *sati bhāvaḥ*). That is, it is the cause because it is after appre-

[1] This is Vācaspati Miśra's interpretation. Uddyotakara's words are: *anabhyupagatārthāntara-viśeṣasya ca hetur vipakṣād viśeṣa iti* (*NV*, p. 124, l. 16). Vācaspati comments: *anabhyupagateti. anabhyupagato arthāntaraṁ vipakṣo yasya hetor, anityatve sādhye kṛtakatvādeḥ, sa tathoktaḥ* (*NVT*, p. 190, l. 24).

Uddyotakara frequently uses the *argumentum ad hominem* derived from this illustration which the *Bauddha* inconsistently gives as an illustration of a valid argument.

It is to this present retort against the *Bauddha* that Uddyotakara seems to be referring in the comment on the next *sūtra*: *tad etal lakṣaṇam svasiddhāntenāsaṁgatatvād alakṣaṇam iti tad api hetu-vārttikaṁ kurvāṇenoktam* (*NV*, p. 132, l. 18. Dr. Jhā is clearly mistaken in regarding this, *ad loc.*, as a reference to a *Vārttika* by some *Bauddha* writer. Uddyotakara's comment on *NS*, I, i, 34, which gives the definition of *hetu*, would probably be called the *hetu-vārttika*.)

hension of this likeness that the various factors—intention to say something, effort of will, expulsion of breath, impact of the breath on the palate and other places—become causes of the sound. And so, mediately, the likeness is the cause: and thus the ablative is the better usage."

The account of the controversy in the *Tātparya*.

The passage in which Vācaspati Miśra explains Diṅnāga's criticism is as follows:

NVT, p. 189, l. 16–p. 190, l. 3. *etat kila hetu-lakṣaṇaṁ bhadanto dūṣayāṁ babhūva*

(a) SĀDHANAṀ YADI SĀDHARMYAṀ, NA VĀKYĀṀŚAḤ—

na hy arthaḥ pañcāvayava-vākyasyāvayavaḥ—

(b) NA PAÑCAMĪ—

yadi sādhana-sādharmyayor atyantābhedo, yadi vā sāmānya-viśeṣa-bhāvena kathaṁcid bheda, ubhayathā na pañcamī, sādhana-sāmānādhikaraṇyena prathamā-prasaṅgāt, atyantābhede caikatara-pada-prayogāt. vākyaṁ cet, tataḥ pañcamy upapadyate. sādhanaṁ hi vākyarūpaṁ sādharmyād arthād utthitaṁ, yataḥ tad viśeṣyam syāt. na hi vākyam evārthad utthitam, apitu vivakṣādyapīti.—na viśeṣyaṁ. kutah?
(c) SĀDHANATVĀD ASAMBHAVAḤ. *artha - samutthānāṁ jñāna - vivakṣādīnām aprasaṅgo 'sādhanatvād iti. na tatrāpi dvedhā doṣāt sākṣāt sādhanaṁ pāraṁparyeṇa vā. yadi pāraṁparyeṇa, vaktṛ-jñānaṁ tarhi sākṣāt sādharmya-samutthaṁ, pāraṁparyeṇa ca śrotuḥ sādhya-vijñāna-sādhanaṁ hetuḥ syāt. atha sākṣāt sādhanaṁ, tarhi śrotṛ-jñānaṁ pāraṁparyeṇa sādharmya-sam-*
(d) *utthaṁ sākṣāt sādhanaṁ hetuḥ syāt.* PRAKṚTE TV ANYA-SAMBHAVAḤ. *yadi tu pañcāvayava-vākyasya prakṛtatvāj jñānādi-vyavacchedaḥ, tathāpy* ANYA-SAMBHAVAḤ—*upanayasyāpi sādharmya-samutthatvāt.*

(e) SVALAKṢAṆENA BĀDHĀ CEN, NA, VIKALPĀDI-SAMBHAVĀT

(f) TASMĀT ṢAṢṬHY ASTU TATRĀPI VIŚEṢAṆAM ANARTHAKAM—

sādharmyasya hetur ity etāvan-mātraṁ vaktavyam iti. tad etad Diṅnāga-dūṣaṇam upanyasyati

UDĀHARAṆA-SĀDHARMYĀCC*eti.*

[See also *NVT*, p. 190, ll. 5, 19, and 26.]

Apparent citations are marked by capitals. Those marked (*a*) and (*b*), taken together, form one complete line. Those marked (*c*) and (*d*) appear to be the second halves of two lines. Those marked (*e*) and (*f*) are two complete lines. The fragment thus comprises three whole lines and two half lines. But one more complete line appears to be contained in the citation made by Uddyotakara and referred to in the last clause of the present passage: for, omitting the *ca*, we get—

UDĀHARAṆA-SĀDHARMYĀT KIM ANYAT SĀDHYA-SĀDHANAM. (γ)

The fragment, supplemented by this, which appears to be its first line, amounts to four whole lines and two halves. I cannot disentangle any other metrical fragments from the passage, though it seems probable that others may be concealed in it.

This passage may be translated thus:

"The *Bauddha* criticised this definition. He says: 'If the means of proof *is* the likeness, then (i) it is not a member of the syllogism, and (ii) the ablative—*udāharaṇa-sādharmyāt*—could not be used. It is not a member of the syllogism, because a *thing* cannot be a member of a whole composed of five *statements*. And the ablative is out of place, because, whether you mean to assert *absolute identity* of means of proof with likeness, or to assert that means of proof is a specific case of the generic notion of likeness (so that there is in some sense difference between them), the ablative would be out of place either way. For in the latter case both words *refer to the same thing* (*sāmānādhikaraṇya*), and so the first or nominative case-inflection should be used; and in the former case you would use one or other of the words, but not both of them (you could call the *hetu udāharaṇa-sadharmya*, or you could call it *sādhya-sādhana:* but you would not call it both at once). **Fragments (*a*) and (*b*).**

"It might be said that if the *hetu* is understood as a statement, the ablative then becomes possible. For the means of proof, understood as a proposition, *is* derived from a fact, viz. the likeness between the Subject of inference and the

Example: so that it can be the subject of this qualification (i.e. *sādhana*, in the sense of a proposition, can be qualified as 'derived from the likeness'). Of course it is not only the statement, but also the intention to say something and so on, that is derived from the likeness. And, taken in this way, *sādhana* cannot be the subject of the qualification *udāharaṇa-*

Fragment (c). *sādharmyāt*. Why? It is impossible[1] because the *sādhana* *is* the *sādhana*, *i.e.* the means of proving what is to be proved: while this would not be true of what *arises from the fact*, viz. the knowledge of the fact, the intention to assert it, and so on, these are *not* the means of proving what is to be proved (*i.e.* the fact itself is the *sādhana;* what can be characterised as '*arising from* the fact' is, for that very reason, not the *sādhana*). Nor can you take *sādhana* in a double sense here, as directly or immediately the means of proof, on the one hand; and as indirectly or mediately means of proof, on the other hand: for either way involves difficulties. Taking the Reason to be what is *indirectly* the means of proving the conclusion, then it is the speaker's knowledge—directly derived from the likeness—that is *indirectly* the means of establishing knowledge of the probandum in the mind of the hearer: and it is therefore the *speaker's* knowledge which should be the 'reason' for the *hearer's* conclusion (which is patently absurd). And, taking the Reason to be what is *directly* the means of proving the conclusion, then the hearer's knowledge—*indirectly* derived from the likeness—is *directly* the means of proving the conclusion for him, and it is therefore the hearer's knowledge that is the Reason (which will not consist with your definition, according to which the Reason is *derived from the likeness*: but the hearer's knowledge is *not* derived from the likeness, but from the speaker's statement). (The *Naiyāyika* is apparently supposed to retort at this point that he is not talking about 'knowledge,' whether of the speaker or of the hearer. He is talking about 'Reason'

[1] Or, 'the *sādhana* does not arise (*sambhava*) from the likeness, just because it *is* the *sādhana*.'

in the context of the syllogism or 'five-membered *statement*'; and, as part of the five-membered *statement*, the 'Reason' must be taken to be itself neither more nor less than a *statement*. To this Diṅnāga replies:) Taking the 'Reason' in the strict sense determined by the context, *i.e.* as a *statement*, so as to exclude the knowledge of speaker and hearer and so forth, your definition is still open to the objection that other things as well are 'derived from the likeness': for the Application, or fourth member of your syllogism, is also 'derived from the likeness of the Subject to the example' (seeing that this likeness is the very thing which is stated in the fourth member —*tathā cāyam*)." Fragment (*d*).

(Vācaspati now cites two complete lines, which seem to mean:)

"If it be said that the view that the means of proof is the thing itself, is contradicted by the *Bauddha* theory of the thing as being the *ding-an-sich* or unique particular, this is not so, because there arise 'fictions of the understanding' (which somehow correspond to the *ding-an-sich*: and these fictions comprise the 'likeness' which serves as the probans in inference). Fragment (*e*).

"The *Naiyāyika* might reply to certain of the above criticisms by saying that the possessive case might be substituted for the ablative (*udāharaṇa-sādharmyasya* in place of *udāharaṇa-sādharmyāt*). The reply to this is that in that case also the qualification (*sādhya-sādhanam*) has no meaning" (because, as Vācaspati says, it is put as qualification of the *statement* of likeness—*NVT*, p. 190, l. 19. So that the objection remains—you cannot qualify the statement *of* the likeness as 'probative,' any more than you can qualify the statement arising *from* the likeness as 'probative'). Fragment (*f*).

(Vācaspati concludes:) "It is this criticism made by Diṅnāga that the *Vārttika* refers to in the passage beginning UDĀHARAṆA-SĀDHARMYĀC CA."

The line cited by Uddyotakara at the opening of the passage on which Vācaspati is commenting probably forms the first

Fragment (g). line of the passage in Diṇṇāga—*udāharaṇa-sādharmyāt kim anyat sādhya-sādhanam?* It may be interpreted: "What else is the means of proving the probandum than the likeness to the example itself?" That is: the *Naiyāyika* says 'the Reason is the proof of the *prabandum from* likeness to the example.' The ablative implies that the means of proof is *other* than the likeness. But the likeness *is* the means of proof.

SECTION 18.—**Fragment M**: DEFINITION OF THE '*Probans*,' '*Hetu*' (as a term in the inference: not as a 'member' of the '*pañcāvayava-vākya*').

Fragment (incomplete line). GRĀHYA-DHARMAS TAD-AṀŚENA VYĀPTO HETUḤ . . .

NV, p. 134, l. 13. *etena grāhya-dharmas tad-aṁśena vyāpto*[1] *hetur iti pratyuktam. anenāvyāpakādir labhyata ity*[2] *uktottaram etad apīti.*

NVT, p. 199, l. 9. *Diṅnāgasyaiva pradeśāntara-hetu-lakṣaṇam. grāhya-dharmaḥ pakṣa-dharmaḥ. tad-aṁśena tasyaiva pakṣasyāṁśena sādhya-dharma-sāmānyena vyāpto hetur iti. tad eva tad-dhetu-lakṣaṇam upanyasyā 'smin pūrvoktaṁ doṣaṁ atidiśati eteneti. atideśam eva sphuṭayati avyāpakādir iti. yathā-śruta-lakṣaṇe pakṣāvyāpakasya hetutvaṁ tad-aṁśetivyāptam ity*[3] *asya vivaraṇālocanena sapakṣa-sattvaṁ vipakṣāc ca vyāvṛttir ity arthaḥ. tathā ca pūrvokta-doṣa-prasaṅga ity arthaḥ.*

That is: Uddyotakara says:

"By this the definition of the reason as 'a quality of the subject (S) which is pervaded (universally accompanied) by

[1] The text has the meaningless *vyāptyor*, but the editor notes that *NVT* has *vyāpto*, which is certainly the right reading.

[2] The text reads *iti* (without *saṁdhi*). Printed texts are not always consistent in their application of *saṁdhi*. I think the two clauses should run together, and I have therefore inserted the *saṁdhi*.

[3] Read *tad-aṁśena vyāpta ity* in place of the textual *tad-aṁśeti-vyāptam ity*, which seems to be meaningless.

an aspect (P) of the subject (S)', is set aside. That is, this definition also has been answered: the answer being that it would apply to middle terms which do not reside in the whole of the Subject, and so on."

Vācaspati comments on this:

"A definition of the reason given by Diṇnāga himself in another place. The word *grāhya-dharma* in this definition means *pakṣa-dharma*, 'a quality of the *pakṣa* or Subject of inference. *Tad-aṁśena:* this means *tasya*, i.e. *pakṣasya*, *aṁśena:* that is, *sādhya-dharma-sāmānyena*—the reason is pervaded by the general nature of the quality which is to be proved (by P, as a universal). He cites the definition, and extends the application of the previous criticism to it, in the words 'By this,' etc. He explains how that criticism applies to this definition in the words 'it would apply to middle terms which do not reside in the whole of the subject.' Taking the definition as it stands, a middle which did not reside in the whole of S would be a reason (*i.e.* a valid middle term). Reference to the explanation ('*Vivaraṇa*,' which may mean Diṇnāga's own *Vṛtti* on the *Pramāṇa-samuccaya*) will show that the words *tad-aṁśena vyāptaḥ* mean residence in the *sapakṣa* and absence from the *vipakṣa:* so that the criticisms previously brought against Diṅnāga's conception of the *trairūpya* and of *tri-lakṣaṇa-hetu* (see fragments H and J and K above) are also applicable to this definition."

Vidyābhūṣaṇa does not notice this fragment, and it is difficult to locate it. But for the explicit statement of Vācaspati that it comes from 'another place,' it would have been natural to connect it with fragments J and K, and refer it to Chapter III of the *Pramāṇa-samuccaya*. In view of Vācaspati's statement, however, it has to be assigned either to another work altogether (which is improbable, as Vācaspati's other citations all seem to come from the *Pramāṇa-samuccaya*): or else either to Chapter II, which discusses inference for oneself, or to Chapter IV, in connection with the discussion or

Identification.

hetu as a member of the *pañcāvayava-vākya*. The attribution to Chapter II appears most probable.

The fragment is important because in it (and in it alone) the doctrine of *vyāpti*—with which Diṅnāga's name is always connected—is explicitly stated: and stated in language parallel to that used by Kumārila. The use of *aṁśa* seems to be identical with Kumārila's use of *ekadeśa* when he speaks of the *pakṣa* (S) as the *ekadeśin* or *ekadeśavat*, which has as its two *ekadeśas* the *gamaka* or *hetu* (M) on the one hand, and the *gamya* or *sādhya* (P) on the other hand. The phraseology in which Vācaspati explicates it is reminiscent rather of Praśastapāda: *cf.* what is said of the *nidarśana* (=*udāharaṇa*, third member of the 'syllogism') in *Praśastapāda-bhāṣya*, p. 251, *anena sādhya-sāmānyena sādhana-sāmānyasyā 'nugama-mātram ucyate.*

The *vyāpti* doctrine is ultimately inconsistent with the view of inference as an affair of examples, embodied in the *trairūpya* doctrine. But both doctrines played a prominent part in Diṅnāga's logic. He is said to have originated the former doctrine: but probably he inherited the *trairūpya* doctrine from predecessors; and Sugiura states that he himself in the *Nyāya-dvāra* ascribes it to 'Soomook,' *i.e.* to Akṣapāda,[1] the reputed author of the *Nyāya Sūtra*. But it does not figure in the *Nyāya Sūtra*, though it seems to be implicit in one sūtra of the fifth chapter (*NS*, V, i, 34), and (more clearly) in Vātsyāyana's *bhāṣya* thereon.

SECTION 19.—**Fragment N**: 'COMPARISON' (*Upamāna*) IS ONLY THE PERCEPTION OF LIKENESS, OR OF AN OBJECT AS LIKE, AND IS THEREFORE NOT A SEPARATE SOURCE OF KNOWLEDGE ('*Pramāṇa*').

NV, p. 60, l. 16. *pratyakṣāgamābhyāṁ nopamānaṁ bhidyate. katham iti? yadā tāv ubhau go-gavayau pratyakṣeṇa*

[1] For the identification of 'Soomook' of the Chinese tradition with Akṣapāda or Gautama, see Sugiura, *Buddhist Logic as preserved in China and Japan* (Philadelphia, 1900, p. 21, footnote 3).

paśyati, tadā hy ayam "anena sarūpa" iti pratyakṣataḥ pratipadyate. yadāpi śṛṇoti "yathā gaur evaṁ gavaya" iti, tadāsya śṛṇvata eva buddhir upajāyate "kecid godharmā gavaye 'nvayina upalabhyante, kecid vyatirekiṇa" iti—anyathā hi yathā tathety eva na syāt—bhūyas tu sārūpyaṁ gavā gavayasyety (text: *gavayasya iti*) *evaṁ pratipadyate. Tasmān nopamānaṁ pratyakṣāgamābhyāṁ bhidyata iti. gavā gavaya-sādṛśyaṁ pratipadyate, gavaya-sattāṁ veti. aho pramāṇābhijñatā Bhadantasya. gavā gavaya-sārūpya-pratipattes tu sañjñā-sañjñi-saṁbandhaṁ pratipadyata iti sūtrārthaḥ. tasmād aparijñāya sūtrārthaṁ yatkiñcid ucyate.*

NVT, p. 135, l. 2. *tad īdṛśam upamāna-phalam avidvān sādṛśya-jñānaṁ sādṛśya-viśiṣta-jñānaṁ vopamāna-phalam iti bhrānto Bhadanto Diṅnāga ākṣipati: pratyakṣeti.*

Ibid., l. 14. *tasmān na sādṛśya-pratīti-phalam upamānaṁ* Fragment ? *pratyakṣād vakyād va vyatiricyata iti sūktam. Bhadanta-bhrāntim udghāṭayati: gaveti.*

That is, Uddyotakara says:

"'Comparison is not distinct from perception and testimony.' How so? Because when a person *sees* both the cow and the gayal, in that case it is by perception that he apprehends that this is like that: and when he is *told* that the gayal is like the cow, in that case it is just on the hearing of this that the knowledge arises in his mind that some of the qualities of the cow are found in the gayal and others are not: as otherwise the word 'like' would not have been used by the speaker: and he apprehends a preponderant sameness of the qualities of the gayal with those of the cow. For this reason 'comparison is not distinct from perception and testimony.' On this account of the matter, what the person apprehends is (in the latter case) the resemblance of the cow to the gayal, or (in the former case) the existence of the gayal (as qualified by resemblance to the cow). What understanding the *Bauddha* shows of the nature of the *pramāṇa!* (that is, he has altogether misunderstood the sense in which *upamāna* is asserted to be a *pramāṇa*). The *sūtra* really means that, as a result of apprehending the resemblance of the gayal to the cow, the person realises the relation of the name 'gayal' to this particular object. Therefore, what is urged is irrelevant, and arises from ignorance of what the *sūtra* means."

Vācaspati's comment means:

"The *Bauddha*—that is, Diṅnāga—raises the objection, 'comparison is not distinct from perception and testimony,' because he did not understand that the resultant cognition produced by *upamāna* (considered as a separate *pramāṇa*) is such as we have explained it to be; and because he mistakenly thought that the knowledge of the likeness, or of an object qualified by the likeness, is the *resultant* cognition produced by *upamāna* (whereas in fact these constitute the *means* of a further cognition)."

And again:

"Therefore (the *Bauddha* concludes) 'it is not well said that comparison is separate from perception or testimony.' Uddyotakara explains the *Bauddha's* mistake in the words 'as a result of apprehending the likeness of the gayal to the cow,'" etc.

Identification. Vidyābhūṣaṇa, *HIL*, p. 287, n. 2, cites as from Chapter IV of the *Pramāṇa-samuccaya* a line in connection with Diṅnāga's rejection of *upamāna* as a separate source of knowledge. Uddyotakara and Vācaspati appear to cite Diṅnāga in different versions. Possibly Vācaspati's *nopamānam pratyakṣād vakyād vā vyatiricyate* is actual citation, of which Uddyotakara's *pratyṣāgamābhyāṁ nopamānaṁ bhidyate* is a paraphrase.

It seems surprising that Diṅnāga should have interpreted the *sūtra* (*NS*, I, i, 6) in disregard of Vātsyāyana's interpretation of it, as he appears to have done. Of course the interpretation of the *sūtra*, taken in itself, is doubtful: and a later passage (*NS*, II, i, 44-48) can perhaps just as well be cited to support Diṅnāga's as to support Vātsyāyana's interpretation of I, i, 6. The orthodox *Naiyāyika* account of *upamāna* does in fact read like an afterthought, and it is difficult to believe that it represents the original teaching of the *sūtra*. I am inclined to think that the acceptance of *upamāna* as a separate *pramāṇa* is connected with the acceptance of the *upanaya* as a fourth member of syllogism. *NS*, II, i, 48 appeals to the linguistic usage of *yathā . . . tathā* as evidence that *upāmana* is a separate *pramāṇa ;* and this suggests the *tathā cāyam* which is the formula of the *upanaya*. Moreover, the phraseology of that *sūtra—tathety upasaṁhārāt*—seems to invite reference to the *sūtra* (*NS*, I, i, 38) which defines *upanaya—udāharaṇāpekṣas tathety upasaṁhāro na tatheti vā sādhyasyopanayaḥ*. And finally Vātsyāyana himself, in a passage which may embody the older doctrine, definitely identifies the *upanaya* with *upamāna* (*NBh*, p. 44, l. 13, *upamānam upanayaḥ tathety upasaṁharāt*). Therefore what Diṅnāga criticises may really have been the doctrine of the *sūtrakāra*, which the school later found it convenient to interpret in a different, and rather forced, sense.

SECTION 20.—**Fragment O** : THE OBJECT OF INFERENCE IS AN IDEAL CONSTRUCTION.

(1) *NVT*, p. 127, l. 1. *vastu-vacane 'py artha-śabdasya lakṣyāsaṁbhavād aviṣayaṁ lakṣaṇam. na hi Diṅnāga-mate kiṁcid asti vastu yan nāntarīyakaṁ sad-dhetur bhavati: yathā 'ha—*

Fragment (prose).

SARVO 'YAM ANUMĀNĀNUMEYA-BHĀVO BUDDHYĀRŪḌHENA DHARMA-DHARMI-BHĀVENA NA BAHIḤ SAD-ASATTVAM APEKṢATE

—iti.

(2) *NVT*, p. 39, l. 12. *tathā cāgamānusaṁdhānena pratijñāyāḥ kalpita-viṣayatvam api nirākṛtaṁ veditavyam, yadā 'hur eke—*

SARVO 'YAM ANUMĀNĀNUMEYA-VYAVAHĀRO BUDDHYĀRŪḌHENAIVA DHARMA-DHARMI-BHĀVENA NA BAHIḤ SAD-ASATTVAM APEKṢATE

—iti.

(3) *Śloka-vārtika*, *nirālambana-vāda*, 167-168.

nanv asaty api bāhye 'rthe buddhyārūḍhena[1] *sidhyati*
vāsanā-śabda-bhedottha-vikalpa-pravibhāgataḥ.

[1] The text has, mistakenly, *buddhyārūḍhe na*. Jhā's translation implies *buddhyārūḍhena*.

nyāya-vidbhir idaṁ coktaṁ dharmādau buddhim āśrite
vyavahāro 'numānādeḥ kalpyate na bahiḥ-sthite.

Pārthasārathi Miśra's *Nyāyaratnākara, ad loc.*

vṛddhānām apy asmadīyānām idam evā 'bhimatam ity āha nyāya-vidbhir iti.

SARVA EVĀ 'NUMANANUMEYA-VYAVAHĀRO BUDDHYĀRŪḌHENA DHARMA-DHARMI-NYĀYENA NA BAHIḤ-SATTĀM APEKṢATA

iti Diṅnāgenoktam iti.

Context and translation.

1. Vācaspati is referring to the passage in Uddyotakara's comment on *NS*, I, i, 5, in which a criticism is given of Diṅnāga's definition of *anumāna* as *nāntarīyakārtha-darśanaṁ tad-vidaḥ* (fragment G, above). As against this definition he brings the following *argumentum ad hominem* (not adduced by Uddyotakara): "Since the word '*artha*' signifies a *real* thing, the definition has nothing to which it can refer: because the thing defined cannot exist. For on Diṅnāga's view there is no real thing which could be 'inseparably connected with the *probandum*' so as to be a valid reason. As he has said:

"'This whole business of *probans* and *probandum* depends on the relation of quality and possessor of quality—a relation which is imposed by thought; and it has no reference to an external existence and non-existence.'"

2. Vācaspati is here referring to Uddyotakara's comment (*NV*, p. 17, ll. 14-18) on Vātsyāyana's statement *āgamaḥ pratijñā*—'The Proposition is testimony' (*NBh*, p. 5, l. 3 on *NS*, I, i, 1). The objection is made that the Proposition is something *to be* proved; whereas if it has the authority of 'testimony'—which is an independent *pramāṇa*—it would be *already* proved. Uddyotakara replies that there is nothing to prevent a man's conveying to another as a reasoned truth what he himself accepts as established by authority. Vācaspati adds that this applies to the fundamental truths which it is the function of the *Nyāya* as a system to convey: but that Vātsyāyana does not mean that in all inferences the propo-

sition is 'testimony.' He then adds: "And by his thus connecting the Proposition with testimony it is to be understood that the reference of the proposition to a suppositious subject is rejected: since certain persons have said: 'This whole business of *probans* and *probandum* depends on nothing but the relation of quality and quality-possessor—a relation merely imposed by thought; and does not refer to external existence and non-existence.'"

3. Kumārila is arguing that the *Bauddha* sceptic who maintains all things (including the means of proof themselves) to be unreal, cannot consistently use reasoning to establish his position. The *Bauddha* suggests in reply that a relative or merely phenomenal reality (*saṃvṛti*) provides the sceptic with all that he needs:

"Even though no external object exists, conclusions are established by means of what is merely imposed by the understanding, as the result of differentiating those fictions of the understanding which arise from 'impressions' (mental dispositions) and from (the use of) language. And (our) logicians have said: 'The *probans*, etc., work on qualities, etc., which are grounded in thought and have no external existence.'"

Pārthasārathi Miśra's comment on this is:

"'Our logicians have said': That is, our ancient writers have maintained this very position. Thus Diṅnāga says: 'This *whole* (*sarva eva*) business of *probans* and *probandum* depends on the relation of quality and quality-possessor—a relation imposed by thought; and it does not refer to external existence.'"

See Keith, *ILA*, p. 102, n. 2; he refers to passages (1) and (3). Identification.
Vidyābhūṣaṇa does not appear to have noted this fragment. It is even better accredited than the rest of these fragments, as both Vācaspati and Pārthasārathi attribute it to Diṅnāga by name. The fact that Kumārila deals with it in the *nirālambana-vāda* suggests that the fragment may be found in Diṅnāga's *Ālambana-parīkṣā*, or in his *vṛtti* thereon.

Keith's statement that Diṅnāga "emphatically denies that

there can be any real thing indissolubly connected" is an inadvertence. It is Vācaspati who denies that—on Diṅnāga's view—there can be any indissoluble connection of real things. This point has some importance in view of the fact that Stcherbatsky and Keith both argue that Diṅnāga's idealistic position provided him with a basis for the doctrine of indissoluble connection: of which doctrine he is, partly on that ground, supposed to be the originator. See Keith, *ILA*, pp. 103-104. "*A priori*, therefore, it is more reasonable to assume that Praśastapāda owes the principle" (of indissoluble connection) "to a school in which it had a natural right to exist." The fact is that the *Naiyāyika*, so far from admitting that the principle has a natural right to exist in an idealistic system, emphatically denies that such a system has any right to such an idea. And I think there is no evidence that Diṅnāga himself ever bases his doctrine of indissoluble connection on his idealism

SECTION 21.—**Fragment P**: DEFINITION OF DISCUSSION (*Vāda*)

NV, p. 124, l. 8. *svayaṁ vacana-viśeṣakāni bahūni vākyāni prayuktāni. tad yathā—*

Diṅnāga's definition. SVA-PARA-PAKṢAYOḤ SIDDHY-ASIDDHY-ARTHAṀ VACANAṀ VĀDA —*iti.*

(For translation and context see fragment L, p. 39, above. Vācaspati adds nothing material in his comment here. But the fragment raises a problem: because in a later passage the *Vārttika* cites and criticises in great detail another *almost* identical definition, which Vācaspati Miśra, in his comment *ad loc.*, definitely attributes to 'Subandhu'—*i.e.*, presumably, Vasubandhu. The passages referred to are as follows:)

'Subandhu's' definition. *NV*, p. 151, l. 20. *apare tu sva-para-pakṣa-siddhy-asiddhy-arthaṁ vacanaṁ vāda iti vāda-lakṣaṇaṁ varṇayanti.*

NVT, p. 218, l. 9. *tad evaṁ svābhimatam vāda-lakṣaṇaṁ*

vyākhyāya SAUBANDHAVAṀ *lakṣaṇaṁ dūṣayitum upanyasyati apare tv iti.*

The definition is not explicitly attributed to Diṅnāga, but the context leaves no room for doubt that Vācaspati intends the attribution. It is clear that Diṅnāga's definition is merely an amended version of Vasubandhu's, the amendment consisting in breaking up the compound *sva-para-pakṣa-siddhy-asiddhy-artham* into *sva-para-pakṣayoḥ siddhy-asiddhy-artham.*[1] **Identification.**

Uddyotakara's point against Diṅnāga's amended formula is that nothing is gained by the uncompounded form which Diṅnāga substitutes for the compound *sva-para-pakṣa-siddhy-asiddhy-artham.* For instance, even when the compound is thus resolved the definition remains open to the objection that the phrase 'proving and disproving one's own and the other party's position' leaves it undecided which of the two is to be proved and which disproved. And if you say that the one sense is inevitable because the other is plainly impossible, then you *ought* to use the compound. Why? Because your *vādābhidhāna*[2] is reckoned as *śāstra*, and you cannot—in reference to *śāstra*—say that parsimony in expression is of no account. **Uddyotakara's criticism.**

The commentators on the present *sūtra* (*NS*, I, ii, 1—definition of *vāda*) are writing with direct reference to some Buddhist text which is regarded as of primary authority (*śāstratvenābhyupagata*), and is so well known that Uddyotakara refers to one of its '*sūtras*' by citing merely the first two

[1] Jhā's translation inadvertently cites the *saubandhavaṁ lakṣaṇam* in the uncompounded form, thereby making it identical with Diṅnāga's definition (transl., vol. i, p. 441).

[2] *NV*, p. 156, l. 17. *śāstratvena ca vādābhidhānam abhyupagamyate, na ca varṇe guru-lāghavam āśrīyata iti na yuktam.* Dr. Jhā relies on this passage to establish his contention that 'Subandhu' wrote the *Vāda-vidhi* or *Vāda-vidhāna* referred to at *NV*, p. 121, l. 2 (see his notes at pp. 441 and 454 of vol. i of translation). He supports his view by the ingenious emendation *vāda-vidhānam* for *vādābhidhānam* in the present passage. But, apart from this emendation, his view is probably correct: see above, p. 26. *vādābhidhānam* need not be altered. It would mean: "the definition of *vāda* is reckoned as *śāstra*." But the emendation is tempting.

words—*sādhana-dūṣaṇair ity etasmin sūtre* (*NV*, p. 154, l. 3).

Another fragment of Vasubandhu?

Vācaspati gives the full *sūtra*—*te sādhana-dūṣaṇaih sva-para-śabdāḥ sambadhyante*, "the words *sva-* and *para-* are connected with proving and refuting" (*NVT*, p. 219, l. 13). This '*sūtra*' is clearly explanatory of the definition of *vāda* here criticised: and that definition is itself called a '*sūtra*'[1] by Uddyotakara (*laghu ca sūtraṁ bhavati*—*NV*, p. 153, l. 15). Further, Vācaspati cites a '*gāthā*': *nāsti prayojanād iṣṭaṁ mukhya-śabdārtha-laṅghanam*—*iti gāthā bhavatām*. "You have a verse: 'it is not permissible to depart from the primary meaning of a word (arbitrarily ?).'"

It would be a matter of some importance to identify these citations. They may come from the *vāda-vidhi* referred to by Uddyotakara on *NS*, I, i, 33, in connection with the definition of *pratijñā*: and the *vāda-vidhi* may be the work of Vasubandhu. More can hardly be said. But who was the author of the *vāda-vidhāna-ṭīkā*, also mentioned by Uddyotakara in the same connection (*NV*, p. 120, l. 6)? Was it Diṅnāga? If not, in what work is Diṅnāga's amendment of 'Subandhu's' definition of *vāda* (and of *pratijñā*, perhaps) to be found?

SECTION 22.—**Fragment Q**: CRITICISM OF THE 'VAIŚEṢIKA' ACCOUNT OF THE UNIVERSAL (*Sāmānya*).

Sarva-darśana-saṁgraha, *Bauddha-darśana* (=Cowell and Gough, p. 21).

Tad uktam—

Fragment.

ANYATRA VARTAMĀNASYA TATO 'NYA-STHĀNA-JANMANI
TASMĀD ACALATAḤ STHĀNĀD VṚTTIR ITY ATIYUKTATĀ
YATRĀ 'SAU VARTATE BHĀVAS TENA SAṀBADHYATE NA TU
TADDEŚINAṀ CA[2] VYĀPNOTI KIM APY ETAN MAHĀDBHUTAM.[3]
NA YĀTI NA CA TATRĀ 'SĪD ASTI PASCĀN NA CĀṀŚAVAT
JAHĀTI PŪRVAṀ NĀDHĀRAM AHO VYASANA-SAṀTATIḤ.

[1] Similarly at *NV*, p. 43, l. 14, Uddyotakara speaks of Vasubandhu's definition of perception as a '*sūtra*'—*yadyapy etat sūtraṁ yathāśruti bhavati*, etc.

[2] NA (Poussin).

[3] Poussin (*Muséon*, n.s. ii, 1901, p. 73, n. 45) says that he thinks it necessary to read *na tu Taddeśinaṁ na vyāpnoti*. He renders: "Où

"It has been said: Translation.

'It is great dexterity that what resides in one place should, without moving from that place, reside in what comes to exist in a place other than that place.

'It is joined with this thing (which is now coming into existence) in the place where the thing in question is; and yet it does not fail to pervade the thing which is in *that* place.[1] Is not this very wonderful?

'It does not *go* there—and it was not there before; and yet it is there afterwards—although it is not manifold, and does not quit its former receptacle! What a series of difficulties!'"

Context. *SDS, loc. cit.*

The *Bauddha*, expounding the tenet of the momentariness of the existent as such—*yat sat, tat kṣaṇikam*—gives as a definition of existence *artha-kriyā-kāritva*, practical efficiency. (The argument is that the existent is what *does something:* the permanent can do nothing, because causality is inconsistent with permanence:[2] therefore the existent is non-permanent—momentary.) In this connection he proceeds to deal with a rival theory of the nature of existence, which he attributes to the followers of 'Kaṇabhakṣa and Akṣacaraṇa'—Kaṇāda and Akṣapāda, *i.e.* the *Vaiśeṣikas* and *Naiyāyikas*. This theory is that to exist means to be united with the universal 'Being'—*sattā-sāmānya-yogitvam eva sattvam.* The *Bauddha* makes the obvious retort that this will exclude from existence

que se trouve l'être nouveau, il lui est inhérent; et ne cesse pas, pour cela, d'occuper l'objet qui est ici." The emendation may be accepted as almost certainly correct.

[1] Poussin renders: "Il ne s'en va pas (d'ici), il n'était pas là, il n'est pas multiple après (sa second manifestation), il ne quitte pas son premier receptacle." For a variant of the fifth line of the fragment, see below, p. 59.

[2] Because a permanent cause would produce its effects all at once, there being no reason why it should postpone the production of its effects (*samarthasya kṣepāyogāt.—NVT*, p. 388, l. 17). And if you say that it will produce a given effect when an 'auxiliary circumstance' (*sahakārin*) is added to it, then you are giving up the notion of permanent causal entities and adopting the *Bauddha* doctrine of *kurvadrūpa*, *i.e.* of a *momentary* collocation of circumstances as the cause.

three of the six *Vaiśeṣika* categories, viz. *sāmānya*, *viśeṣa*, and *samavāya* (since the *Vaiśeṣika* himself teaches that 'universals' cannot inhere in universals, or in ultimate differences, or in inherence-relations, but only in substances, qualities, and actions): so that we shall not be able to predicate existence of universals, ultimate differences, or inherences. The *Vaiśeṣika* answers that these three categories have existence predicated of them in a peculiar sense, each of them having an existence *sui generis* (*tatra svarūpa-sattā-nibandhaḥ sad-vyavahāraḥ*).[1] The *Bauddha* objects to this multiplication of meanings of 'existence,' and says that the theory would be confuted by a dilemma of which the two horns are (1) that universal 'Being' does 'run through' everything, (2) that it does not run through everything.[2] As a matter of fact, we do not find any one common presentational form running through things as different as a mountain and a mustard-seed (*anugatasya ākārasya apratibhāsanāt*). Then, again, the *Bauddha* asks, is the universal ubiquitous, or only ubiquitous within its own sphere (*sarva-gataṁ svāśraya-sarva-gataṁ vā*)? The first alternative would mean confusion of all things: besides, Praśastapāda himself says *sva-viṣaya-sarva-gatam*[3]—'ubiquitous in its proper subjects.' Now this second alternative, adopted by Praśastapāda, gives rise to a dilemma:[4] when the universal 'being-a-jar' which resides in an already existing jar is joined to a jar elsewhere which is coming into being, does it go from the first jar to be joined to the second, or is it joined to the second without going from the first? In the first alternative, it would be a substance (for only substances are capable of

[1] This is Praśastapāda's solution. Cf. *PBh*, p. 19, *sāmānyādīnāṁ trayāṇāṁ svātma-sattvam*—the three categories, universality, etc., have their own nature for their being.

[2] This seems to be the meaning of *anugatatvānanugatatva-vikalpa-parāhateḥ*.

[3] *proktaṁ Praśastapādena sva-viṣaya-sarva-gatam iti*. The phrase will be found in *PBh*, p. 314, l. 20. The explicit reference in the *DS* passage to Praśastapāda is noteworthy, for it *may* imply that this fragment from Diṅnāga is directed specifically against Praśastapāda.

[4] What follows explains the fragment from Diṅnāga.

movement, *karma*): and in the second alternative it could not be joined to the second jar.[1] Further, either the universal continues to subsist after the jar has been destroyed—or it perishes—or it goes somewhere else. In the first alternative there will be a universal without any place to reside in; in the second, it is improper to give to the universal the epithet 'eternal' (as the *Vaiśeṣika* does); in the third, it would be a substance (for the reason given above).[2] The theory of the 'universal' is swallowed up by these objections as the moon in an eclipse is swallowed by the demon Rāhu, and is therefore baseless. As has been said——. (Here follows the fragment from Diṅnāga.)

Vidyābhūṣaṇa (*HIL*, pp. 273-274 footnote) quotes from Chapter III of the *Nyāya-dīpikā* of the *Jaina* logician Dharmabhūṣaṇa the following: **Identification.**

na yāti na ca tatrāste na paścād asti nāṁśavat
jahāti pūrvaṁ nādhāram aho vyasana-saṁtatiḥ

—iti Diṅnāga-dūṣita-dūṣaṇa-gaṇa-prasara-prasaṅgāt. "'It does not go, it does not stay, it does not exist afterwards, it has no parts, it does not leave its former receptacle—what a congeries of defects!' because this swarm of objections urged by Diṅnāga issue out of it . . ." (the theory of the universal must be rejected).

The attribution to Diṅnāga is explicit, and there is no reason to doubt its accuracy. The fragment may, perhaps, come from the fifth chapter of the *Pramāṇa-samuccaya*, which treats of the *apoha-vāda*; but Vidyābhūṣaṇa does not identify it with any passage in the Tibetan.

It might be argued that (1) the *SDS* appears to imply that Diṅnāga is referring to Praśastapāda, (2) that if Praśastapāda had been later than Diṅnāga he could hardly have

[1] This is the argument of the first two couplets of the fragment.

[2] This is the argument of the last couplet of the fragment. But the correspondence would be more complete (and an unnecessary repetition in the couplet itself would be avoided) if we could interpret the *yāti* of the couplet to mean *vinaśyati*, 'perishes.'

failed to take notice of this rather damaging piece of dialectic But the reference to Praśastapāda in the *SDS* in this connection may only indicate that, by the time of Mādhavācarya, the *Vaiśeṣika* commentators prior to Praśāstapāda had been forgotten, his *Bhāṣya* having superseded earlier commentaries which undoubtedly existed. And Praśastapāda does seem to be conscious of the difficulties involved in the *Vaiśeṣika* doctrine of the real universal, and may have considered that he had met them sufficiently without an explicit polemic against Diṅnāga.[1]

[1] For further evidence as to the chronological relation between Diṅnāga and Praśastapāda, see Appendix I.

APPENDIX I.

THE *Nyāya-praveśa* AND THE *Nyāya-dvāra*, AND THE RELATION OF DIṄNĀGA TO PRAŚASTAPĀDA.

The *Pramāṇa-samuccaya* is without doubt Diṅnāga's work, for passages which Vācaspati Miśra cites and attributes to Diṅnāga by name have been identified by Vidyābhūṣaṇa with passages in the Tibetan version of the *Pramāṇa-samuccaya.* There is no such corroborative evidence for the attribution either of the *Nyāya-praveśa* or of the *Nyāya-dvāra* to Diṅnāga. The former is attributed to him by Tibetan tradition (according to Vidyābhūṣaṇa): but Chinese tradition (according to Sugiura and Ui) attributes it to Śaṁkara Svāmin, making Diṅnāga the author of the *Nyāya-dvāra.* It seems quite clear that the *Nyāya-dvāra* is an earlier work than the *Nyāya-praveśa ;* and there is no reason to doubt the correctness of the Chinese attribution of the *Nyāya-dvāra* to Diṅnāga. That being the case, it is impossible that Diṅnāga should have been the author of the *Nyāya-praveśa.*

Therefore the relation of Praśastapāda to Diṅnāga cannot be argued on the basis of comparison between the *Nyāya-praveśa* and *Praśastapāda-bhāṣya*, except on the assumption that the *Nyāya-praveśa* is identical in teaching with the other two works. This assumption seems, however, to be very largely justified: for there seems to be very little that is original in the *Nyāya-praveśa.* And so Stcherbatsky's earlier (1904) view that Diṅnāga was prior to Praśastapāda may logically be confirmed by comparisons between the *Nyāya-praveśa* and *Praśastapāda-bhāṣya*, even if we arrive at the conclusion that the *Nyāya-praveśa* was compiled later than *Praśastapāda-bhāṣya.* But it is of course safer to rely on comparison with the fragments of the *Pramāna-samuccaya* and with the *Nyāya-dvāra* (so far as the nature of the latter work is known to us from the accounts of Sugiura and Ui).

In what follows I have brought together certain lines of evidence which might be used to argue the relation of the *Nyāya-dvāra* to the *Nyāya-praveśa*, and of Praśastapāda to Diṅnāga.

(*a*) Classification of fallacies of the thesis (*pratijñābhāsa*) in the *Nyāya-dvāra*, *Nyāya-praveśa*, and *Praśastapāda-bhāṣya*, with Uddyotakara's observations[1] thereon:

Nyāya-dvāra.	*Nyāya-praveśa.*	*Praśastapāda.*
1. *pratyakṣa-viruddha* ('sound inaudible').	The same name and example.	*pratyakṣa-viruddha* ('fire cool').

Uddyotakara says that 'sound is inaudible' is not a proper example of *pratyakṣa-viruddha* because it is not by perception but by inference that we know sound to be an object of the organ of hearing. He says the right example is 'fire is cool,' *i.e.* the example given by Praśastapāda. That is to say, he is comparing Praśastapāda with Diṅnāga, to the disadvantage of the latter.

2. *vikalpa-viruddha* (?) ('it is a fine morning'—said when the sun is low in the west).	*anumāna-viruddha* ('pot eternal').	*anumāna-viruddha* ('space dense').

Uddyotakara says that 'the pot is eternal' (it is supposed to be a proposition maintained fallaciously by a *Vaiśesika*, here) ought to be classed under *sva-śāstra-viruddha*. (See No. 4 below.) It will be noted that he mentions the example given in the *Nyāya-praveśa*, and does not refer to that given in the *Nyāya-dvāra ;* but there was nothing to prevent him from referring to developments later than Diṅnāga, and we need not infer that he regarded the *Nyāya-praveśa* as Diṅnāga's —if it is from the *Nyāya-praveśa* that he took this example.

[1] *NV*, p. 116, l. 18 to p. 117, l.14.

3. *prasiddha-viruddha* (?) ('women and money are abominable things').	*loka-viruddha* ('man's head is pure, because it is a part of an animate being,' *or*, 'money is abominable').	Not recognised by Praśastapāda, who, however, inserts as a third rubric:—

Uddyotakara says that what is *prasiddha* must be so by one of the *pramāṇas*, so that there is no room for this as a separate rubric.

		abhyupagata-viruddha (which, however, is equated by Praśastapāda himself with *āgama-viruddha*): 'Brahmans should drink wine.'

Uddyotakara says that 'Brahmans should drink wine' is a proper example of *āgama-viruddha*, whereas the example given by the *Bauddha* of *āgama-viruddha* is not a proper example.

4. *āgama-viruddha* (?) ('sound is eternal' when maintained by a *Vaiśeṣika*).	*āgama-viruddha*[1] ('sound is eternal').	(See No. 3 above.) *sva-śāstra-viruddha* ('effects exist before their production' said by one who maintains the *asat-kārya-vāda*).

Uddyotakara says that for the *Vaiśeṣika* the doctrine of the non-eternity is sound is *not* based on authority but on inference. Therefore the example given by the *Bauddha* is not an example of *āgama-viruddha*, but of *anumāna-viruddha*. If this is to count as an example of *āgama-viruddha*, then 'the pot is eternal' ought also to be classed as *āgama-viruddha*—but the *Bauddha* has given it as an example of *anumāna-viruddha*. The proper example of *āgama-viruddha* is 'Brahmans should drink wine' (which Praśastapāda

[1] I am indebted to Mr. A. B. Dhruva for the information that in the Sanskrit *Nyāya-praveśa* three of the rubrics are *anumāna-viruddha*, *loka-viruddha*, and *āgama-viruddha*.

gives under *abhyupagata-viruddha* = *āgama-viruddha*. See No. 3).

It seems that *sva-śāstra-viruddha* is an innovation in terminology introduced by Praśastapāda. We must suppose that his *abhyupagata-viruddha* was intended as a correction of the *Bauddha* rubric No. 3, while his *sva-śāstra-viruddha* is meant as an improvement on the *Bauddha* rubric No. 4. He presumably meant that the only possible sense of *prasiddha-viruddha* is *āgama-viruddha*; and that the example which the *Bauddha* gives of *āgama-viruddha* ought to be classed separately as *sva-śāstra-viruddha*, as being opposed not to authority merely, but to the reasoning advanced in the *śāstra*.

5. *sva-vacana-viruddha* ('words have no meaning').	*sva-vacana-viruddha* ('my mother is barren').	*sva-vacana-viruddha* ('words have no meaning').

These five rubrics are the only ones recognised by the *Nyāya-dvāra* and by Praśastapāda. But the *Nyāya-praveśa* adds four others:

6.	A thesis with an unaccepted subject: 'God is almighty.'	
7.	A thesis with an unaccepted predicate.	
8.	A thesis with both an unaccepted subject and an unaccepted predicate.	
9.	A thesis universally accepted: 'Fire is warm.'	

Comparison of the three classifications indicates that the *Nyāya-praveśa* supplements the doctrine of the *Nyāya-dvāra*, and that Praśastapāda emends the latter. The inference would seem to be that both the *Nyāya-praveśa* and Praśastapāda were later than the *Nyāya-dvāra*. And there is some probability that Praśastapāda was either earlier than the *Nyāya-praveśa*, or contemporary with the author of that work.

On the other hand, Vidyābhūṣaṇa, Ui, and Stcherbatsky

have all produced evidence which shows that doctrines found in the *Praśastapāda-bhaṣya*, but not found in the *Vaiśeṣika sūtra*, are referred to both by Diṅnāga himself and by Buddhist writers earlier than Diṅnāga. For instance, Vidyābhūṣaṇa (*HIL.*, p. 279 footnote) says that the *Pramāṇa-samuccaya* cites an explanation of the *Vaiśeṣika sūtra* on perception which closely corresponds with Praśastapāda's explanation. There seems to me no room for doubt, in view of the evidence referred to, that there were *Vaiśeṣika* commentators before Praśastapāda, whose comments Praśastapāda embodied in his *Bhāṣya*, and that it is these earlier commentators who are cited and referred to by Diṅnāga and his *Bauddha* predecessors. (There are numerous passages in the *Bhāṣya* in which Praśastapāda makes a brief statement, and then says precisely the same thing in another and amplified form: and the suggestion certainly is that he is commenting on a scholium in these passages.) It seems to me that this alone will explain how Stcherbatsky, in 1904 and in 1924, has been able to produce excellent reasons for holding the contradictory conclusions (1) that Praśastapāda borrowed from Diṅnāga, and (2) that Diṅnāga borrowed, through Vasubandhu, from Praśastapāda. The evidence does in fact prove both theses at once—so long as we assume that Praśastapāda was the first writer to introduce these notions into the *Vaiśeṣika* school. We are forced, then, to give up that assumption, and to suppose that Praśastapāda was a borrower: not, however, from Diṅnāga—though I do not doubt that he sometimes writes with reference to Diṅnāga—but from his predecessors in his own school, whose doctrines Diṅnāga had criticised. This supposition will explain the various evidences which I now adduce.

(*b*) The *Bauddha* doctrine of the five *kalpanās*, and Praśastapāda's five *viśeṣaṇas* (the 'five predicables'), in the theory of perception.

Diṅnāga objects in the *Pramāṇa-samuccaya* that the *Naiyāyika* (Vātsyāyana in the *Nyāya-bhāṣya*, which he is here attacking) failed to connect his doctrine of perception with 'generality, particularity, substance, quality, and action,' although he has borrowed his definition of perception from the *Vaiśeṣikas*. The order in which the five predicables are mentioned agrees with that of the five *viśeṣaṇas* enumerated by Praśastapāda (*Viz.* edn., p. 186) in describing the five types of 'qualified perception': this substance *exists* (*sāmānya*); this substance is *earth-substance* (*viśeṣa*); the cow *has horns* (qualified by *dravya*); the cow is *white* (*guṇa*); the cow *goes* (*karma*). Praśastapāda's account might in fact be a reply to Diṅnāga's sceptical analysis of determinate (*savikalpaka*) perception, which holds that the determinations (*vikalpa*) are mere fictions (*kalpanā*), and that *pure* perception must be *kalpanāpoḍha*, devoid of determinations. Diṅnāga's own list of the five *kalpanās* differs from Praśastapāda's by adding 'name' and by uniting 'generality' and 'particularity' under the single head of *jāti*. But, in view of the obvious relation of the *viśeṣaṇas* to the *Vaiśeṣika* categories, it would hardly be suggested that Praśastapāda borrowed his *viśeṣaṇas* from Diṅnāga's *kalpanās*. Both lists must derive from *Vaiśeṣika* sources.

(*c*) The *trairūpya*.

Any suggestion that the three 'canons of syllogism' are taken from Buddhist logic is discounted by the fact that Praśastapāda himself cites a couplet which states the doctrine, and which attributes it to '*Kāśyapa*,' *i.e.* to the *Vaiśeṣika* school. The effrontery of such a claim, if the doctrine had really originated recently in the *Bauddha* schools, would be incredible. Moreover, the doctrine is already implicitly present in Vātsyāyana's *Bhāṣya* on *NS*, V, i, 34, and even in that *sūtra* itself. And Sugiura states that the doctrine of the Nine Reasons—which implies and follows from the *trairūpya*—is attributed by Diṅnāga himself to 'Socmock,' *i.e.* Akṣapāda. But the attribution is a little difficult to understand, since Diṅnāga was conversant with the *Nyāya-sūtra*, and there is no explicit formulation therein of the Nine Reasons. Praśastapāda does not give the Nine Reasons, though he recognises two different forms of the valid middle term, as formulated in the Nine Reasons. Possibly Diṅnāga was the first to formalise explicitly the *hetu-cakra*, or Nine Reasons, out of the *trairūpya* doctrine as already developed by *Vaiśeṣika* logic, partly on the basis of the classification of fallacies given by the *Vaiśeṣika-sūtra*. For there is really nothing in the *trairūpya* doctrine which is not contained in the passage of Vātsyāyana just referred to, taken in combination with the classification of fallacies in the *Vaiśeṣika-sūtra*. (The doctrine of *vyāpti* is *not* explicit in the *trairūpya*.) It may be that Diṅnāga, in attributing the Nine Reasons to Socmock, meant merely that it was implicit in the *Nyāya-sūtra*.

(*d*) The controversy about the reality of universals.

The lines cited by the *Sarva-darśana-saṁgraha*, and attributed by a *Jaina* logician to Diṅnāga, attack a *Vaiśeṣika* doctrine of the real universal which is identical with the teaching of Praśastapāda. The *Sarva-darśana-saṁgraha* mentions Praśastapāda by name in the immediate context: and we might be inclined to infer that it was Praśastapāda whom Diṅnāga was attacking—an inference which might be supported by the consideration that Praśastapāda does not reply to Diṅnāga's criticism, as he might have been expected to do if he had written later than Diṅnāga, seeing that the attack is distinctly damaging.

But the doctrine of Praśastapāda is fundamentally that taught in the seventeen *sūtras* which constitute *VS*, I, ii. (Keith has maintained that *VS*, I, ii, 3 teaches the subjectivity of the universal: but it is impossible to maintain this in the face of the explicit statement of *VS*, I, ii, 8, and of the general trend of the section.) There was probably nothing so individual in Praśastapāda's doctrine as to necessitate the supposition that he in particular is the object of Diṅnāga's attack. As to the suggestion that he does not reply, it may be that he considered his own re-statement of the doctrine in itself a sufficient reply—*e.g.*, his statement that universals are ubiquitous each within its proper sphere although they have no local habitation (*aparicchinna-deśa*), that there is a definite totality of conditions (*kāraṇa-sāmagrī-niyama*) requisite for the manifestation of the universal in the individual, and that universals cannot be designated in empty space (*antarāle avyapadeśyāni*) because they cannot reside there either by relation of conjunction (*samyoga*) or by that of inherence (*samavāya*). Prabhākara was able to give a further reply, from which Praśastapāda was precluded by the *Vaiśeṣika* doctrine of the eternity of the *samavāya* relation: "When a new individual belonging to a class is brought into existence, what is brought into existence is not the class-character, which is ever present, but only the relation (inherence) of the individual with that class-character. There is nothing objectionable in the production of inherence, because inherence, according to Prabhākara, is not eternal (as held by the logician)" (Jhā, *PSPM*, p. 100).

(*e*) Real relations as the basis of inference.

Praśastapāda argues against the interpretation of *Vaiśeṣika-sūtra*, IX, ii, 1, as reducing the basis of inference to real relations. This interpretation of the *sūtra* would make it agree with the view of the *Bauddha* logicians, who classify inferences according as they are based on the real relations of causality, and identity (*tadutpatti* and *tādātmya*. The third class was inference by non-perception, *anupalabdhi*). But Praśastapāda does not refer to this Buddhist doctrine, as he might have been expected to do if he had written later than Diṅnāga, who made use of it, and was perhaps the first to do so.

The argument is only from silence. But it would have weight if supported by other lines of evidence.

(*f*) The 'antinomic reason.'

If Diṅnāga was the originator of the conception of the antinomic reason, *viruddhāvyabhicārin*, which is found in the

Nyāya-dvāra, as well as in the *Nyāya-praveśa*, then it is definitely *proved* that Praśastapāda came later: for he refers to the *viruddhāvyabhicārin* by name, and gives reasons for rejecting the conception. This argument has had great weight with me, in the absence of any indication that the *viruddhāvyabhicārin* was mentioned by any writer earlier than Diṅnāga.

(*g*) The conception of inseparable connection, *a-vinā-bhāva* or *vyāpti*.

Sugiura states that the *Nyāya-dvāra* expressly objects to the argument from particular to particular, devoting fully two pages to the subject. Diṅnāga is said to have "introduced a universal proposition to take the place of the old analogical examples." And the doctrine of *vyāpti* seems to be clearly enunciated in the *Pramāna-samuccaya* fragment: *grāhyadharmas tad-aṁśena vyāpto hetuḥ*.

But whether Diṅnāga originated the conception is another question, and so far as I know no evidence has yet been produced to show that it originated in the *Bauddha* rather than in the *Vaiśeṣika* school. It has been very generally assumed that Diṅnāga was its author: but this assumption probably arises from the accident that Uddyotakara, in his powerful attack on the notion of *avinābhāva*, associates the doctrine with Diṅnāga. But this is merely in accordance with his normal habit of ignoring *Vaiśeṣika* logic, where he differs from it, and taking for his opponent the *Bauddha*, whose logical conceptions are very largely identical with those of the *Vaiśeṣika*: for he could not attack the sister-*śāstra* directly. I cannot see any cogent reason for giving Diṅnāga the credit of inventing the doctrine of inseparable connection.

(*h*) Classification of the 'contradictory middle term.'

Praśastapāda gives no divisions of the contradictory reason *viruddha-hetv-ābhāsa*, while the *Nyāya-dvāra* and the *Nyāya-praveśa* both give a fourfold division. This may only show that the *Bauddha* logicians introduced a formal development into the earlier *Vaiśeṣika* logic which they borrowed, and that Praśastapāda was not prepared to accept the innovation.

(*i*) Fallacies of exemplification.

Praśastapāda has a heading here, *āśrayāsiddha*, which is not found in the *Nyāya-dvāra* and the *Nyāya-praveśa;* and his rubrics *lingāsiddha*, *anumeyāsiddha*, and *ubhayāsiddha*, replace (apparently) the terms *liṅga-vyāvṛtta*, *anumeya-vyāvṛtta*, and *ubhaya-vyāvṛtta* of the *Nyāya-dvāra* (see Sugiura, p. 68). And Praśastapāda's terminology is certainly unhappy, because he has already used *ubhayāsiddha* and *anumeyāsiddha* in a different sense as names of two varieties of the *asiddha-hetv-ābhāsa*. If he came after Diṅnāga, he would have been wiser to profit by Diṅnāga's less confusing terminology here. And therefore it might be argued that Diṅnāga came after Praśastapāda and improved on his terminology. This argument seems to me to have considerable weight in itself, but not to outweigh the evidence for the contrary inference. We may credit Praśastapāda here with unwillingness to accept even gifts from the enemy.

(*j*) *Dūṣaṇābhāsa.*

These are the dialectical appearances of refutation, or *jāti*, treated of in the fifth book of the *Nyāya-sūtra*. The *Nyāya-dvāra* gives a list of fourteen, ascribing them to 'Socmock,' *i.e.* Akṣapāda=Gautama. This is another interesting example of the *Bauddha* logicians' consciousness that their logic was only an offshoot of the *Nyāya*. Praśastapāda does not mention *dūṣaṇābhāsa* at all.

No inference as to the relation between Praśastapāda and Diṅnāga can be drawn from this difference. I mention it merely as an indication of the danger of the inferences which we *do* make. For, if we had not known that the doctrine of the *jāti* is given in the *Nyāya-sūtra*, we should not improbably have argued from the silence of Praśastapāda on the subject that he must have been earlier than Diṅnāga.

APPENDIX II.

SUMMARY OF BUDDHIST LOGICAL DOCTRINES REFERRED TO IN THE FRAGMENTS.

There are two sources of knowledge, perception and inference, and not four as the *Naiyāyika* holds. 'Comparison' is only the *perception* of preponderant sameness of qualities in two things (fragment N); or else (so far as our knowledge of the sameness is derived from the statement of another) it is reducible to Testimony. But Testimony again is not a separate source of knowledge, for the *Naiyāyika* defines it as the statement of a credible witness; and our knowledge of the credibility of the witness is derived either from our *perception* of the fact averred by him or from an *inference* as to his credibility drawn from our observation that his other statements have been corroborated (fragment E).

The two *pramāṇas*. **Comparison not a *pramāṇa*.** **Fragment N** **Testimony not a *pramāṇa*.** **Fragment E.**

Perception.

Perception was defined by Vasubandhu as 'knowledge arising from the thing itself' (p. 10, *supra*). This would inevitably raise the problem of distinguishing between the elements which might be regarded as actual presentations and those which seem rather to be accretions contributed by the imagination. Diṅnāga accordingly abstracted the five predicables, namely generic character, specific character, relation to other substances, quality, and action—as 'fictions of the understanding' (*kalpanā*), from the momentary existent (*ksaṇa*, *svalakṣaṇa*) which alone is the object (*grāhya*) of pure perception; and he therefore defined perception as devoid of determinations (*kalpanāpoḍha*). As against such a view the

Perception defined. **Note to Fragment A.** **The 'pure percept.'** **Fragment A.**

Validity of predication.

Vaiśeṣika argued that the five predicables (*viśeṣaṇa*) are given in perception no less than the object itself as qualified by them: there being thus two moments in perception—one consisting in bare intuition (*ālocana-mātra*) of the unrelated characters (*svarūpa*), the other consisting in determinate perception, *i.e.* perception of the object as qualified by the characters. This teaching, first found in the *Bhāṣya* of Praśastapāda, was adopted by the *Nyāya* in the form of the distinction between *nirvikalpaka-pratyakṣa* (approximately equivalent to the 'simple apprehension' of Western logic) and *savikalpaka-pratyakṣa*, or perception of the object as qualified by the characters previously apprehended in the moment of *nirvikalpaka-pratyakṣa*.

It is natural to connect this teaching of the reality of the predicables with the doctrine of the real universal maintained by the *Vaiśeṣika* school, though it must be confessed that the connection is not suggested by Praśastapāda himself,[1] and that the doctrine of the real universal does not appear to be organically related to the *Vaiśeṣika* realism. The universal was treated as a separate category, co-ordinate with substance, quality, action, etc., and was asserted to be eternal and perceptible (*aindriyaka*). Diṅnāga points out the difficulties in such a position (pp. 56-61). The *Bauddha*, reducing reality to unique momentary existents which have nothing in common with each other and of which the identity is constituted merely by the negative conception of excluding what is other (*apoha*), could not, of course, admit real and permanent universals.

Universals unreal. Fragment Q.

Similarly he rejects the *Vaiśeṣika* doctrine of the perceptibility of substance, arguing that it is inconsistent to maintain that colour is the specific object of vision, and at the same time to assert that substance is visible (p. 17). Nor can we be said to have perception of concrete wholes, as the *Naiyāyika* maintains; for perception is 'knowledge arising from the thing itself' (p. 10), while what we call perception of (*e.g.*)

Substance unreal. Fragment D.

[1] It is indicated by the tenth-century commentator, Śrīdhara.

a jar is really a cognition arising (not from the concrete whole as such, but) from colour, etc. (p. 11). The *Bauddha* of course rejects the notion of substance, or of concrete wholes, since for him the existent means the momentary (*yat sat, tat kṣanikam*). And for just this reason his opponents argued that he had no right to the conception of things as indissolubly or universally connected—for on his showing there are no 'things' (*artha*) to be indissolubly connected (pp. 52 and 54).

Criticism of the supposed contact with the object in perception. Fragment C.

The *Nyāya Sūtra* (*NS*, I, i, 4) had defined perception as knowledge arising from contact of sense-organ with object. Diṅnāga points out that on such a view the perception of distance, or of objects larger than the organ of vision, is difficult to explain (pp. 14-16), and that we shall sometimes at least have to admit that the organ functions without getting at the object (*aprāpya-kāritva*, p. 15). The *Nyāya Bhāṣya* had added *manas* to the list of sense-organs involved in perceptual contact, on the authority of the sister-*śāstra*, the *Vaiśeṣika*: perhaps because it is obvious that mere contact of organ of external sense with an object does not give rise to perception, unless the further factor of attention is present. Diṅnāga retorts that the *Nyāya Sūtra* certainly needed a special organ of sense-perception to explain the apprehension of the soul's own states, since these are treated as qualities perceptible in just the same way in which the qualities of external objects are perceived; but that Vātsyāyana's method of supplying the defects of the *sūtra* is hardly satisfactory (pp. 13-14). The *Bauddha* himself does not accept the view that mental states are objects of internal perception (*mānasa-pratyakṣa*), but holds that the passing states are self-conscious (*saṁvedya*, pp. 9-10). Presumably, therefore, he had no use for *manas*.

manas as organ of attention and of inner sense. Fragment B.

Inference.

Inference is drawn through three kinds of inferential 'mark' or middle term, based either on causal relation, or on identity, or on our non-perception of what would have been perceived if present (p. 68). These are of course real relations for the *Vaiśeṣika*, from whom the *Bauddha* borrows them; but, as they are merely ideal constructions for the *Bauddha*, and inconsistent with his view of reality, Vācaspati Miśra seems to

Universal connection is the basis of inference. Fragment G.

be justified in arguing that Diṅnāga has no right to the notion of inseparable connection (*vyāpti*, *avinābhāva*) which he makes the nerve of his doctrine of inference (pp. 52 and 54). The instrument of inference is defined as the experience of a thing which is inseparably connected with another thing when the experiencer is aware of the connection (p. 21); and conformably with this a valid middle term or reason is characterised as a

Fragment M.

property of the Subject which is pervaded by (*vyāpta*), or inseparably connected with, another aspect or property of the Subject (pp. 46-48).

Fragment F.

The *probandum*.

Diṅnāga, Uddyotakara, and Kumārila raise the question: What precisely is the *probandum* in an inference? No doubt the ambiguity of the term *anumeya* or *sādhya* (to which Vātsyāyana had already called attention) suggested the question; but it is not a mere matter of définition of a term, for important logical issues are involved in the answer given. The *prima facie* view is that the property P is the thing-to-be-proved; but plainly this is inadequate, for we are not concerned in an inference with P as such, but with P-in-relation-to-S: and this is the view at which Diṅnāga arrives (pp. 18-21). Uddyotakara's view is difficult to distinguish from this; but he criticises Diṅnāga, apparently on the ground that, starting, as Diṅnāga does, from an abstract connection of P-in-general with M-in-general in the '*vyāpti*' or major premise, it is impossible to arrive in the conclusion at a concrete S-qualified-by-P. We should perhaps express his difficulty by saying that on such a view the syllogism is guilty of *quaternio terminorum:*

M is P,
S is M,
therefore S is SP,

where the particularised P of the conclusion is not identifiable with the P-in-general of the major premise. That is why

Uddyotakara attacks the doctrine that *vyāpti* is the nerve of inference in this context. His own view is that inference is based on the similarity (not identity) between concrete XP and concrete SP, and that M and P can only be connected in a concrete *dharmin*, falling apart when abstracted from the thing which possesses them. He maintains that the *probandum* is a particular case of M as qualified by P—or, symbolised, neither P, nor SP, but SMP. In other words, inference is the passage from XMP to SMP. M is seen to be probative of P in XMP, and inference is the process of *parāmarśa*, through which we see that it is also probative of P in SMP. There is no such thing as abstract connection of properties M and P: inference is from particular to particular, or rather from concrete to concrete, through similarity, *sādharmya*.

'Fourth Figure' conclusions. Kumārila raises the further question whether we can have what we should call a Fourth Figure conclusion. He puts the question in the form: Can we have as our *probandum* P-qualified-by-S (*dharmi-viśiṣṭa-dharma*), or must our *probandum* always be S-qualified-by-P (*dharma-viśiṣṭa-dharmin*)? [1] His answer is that no reasonable meaning can be attached to the Fourth Figure conclusion, P-qualified-by-S.

The paradeigmatic syllogism. Uddyotakara makes a powerful and in part justifiable attack on the doctrine of universal connections between abstract qualities, substituting for *vyāpti* as the nerve of inference the more concrete conception of *parāmarśa*, the connection of properties *in their subject* (*dharmin*). This is in accord with the original teaching of the school, for both the *Sūtra* and the *Bhāṣya* formulate inference as based on the likeness of the case under investigation to examples (*udāharaṇa-sādharmya*), so that the syllogism was paradeigmatic in its earlier formulation, and continued to retain strong traces of its character as an argument from examples even after the *Nyāya* school had adopted the doctrine of *vyāpti* from *Vaiśeṣika-Bauddha* logic.

[1] Vātsyāyana uses these phrases, saying that *sādhya* may have either of these meanings. (*NBh*, p. 41, l. 10 [on *NS*, I, i, 36].)

Thus the Canons of Syllogism, as formulated in the *trairūpya* and in the conception of *trilakṣaṇa hetu*, are essentially an attempt to state the conditions under which similarity to examples constitutes proof; and the Indian syllogism has always retained the habit of mentioning an example in its major premise, and gives the name 'Exemplification' (*udāharaṇa*, *nidarśana*) to that 'member' of the syllogism.

Trairūpya, or Canon of Syllogism. Fragment H.

Diṅnāga's formulation of the *trairūpya* agrees with that cited by Prasastapāda as from an earlier *Vaiśeṣika* writer (p. 23): a valid reason is (i) a property of S, (ii) which is present in cases like S, and (iii) absent in cases unlike S. This teaching merely draws out the implications of the earliest *Naiyāyika* view of inference, though the explicit formulation of it probably came from the *Vaiśeṣika* school, and was no doubt partly suggested by the classification of fallacies as contradictory (*asat*)[1] and inconclusive (*saṁdigdha*) in the *Vaiśeṣika Sūtra;* the former fallacy suggesting the canon of absence in unlike cases, the latter that of presence in (only) like cases. Uddyotakara criticises the formulation of the *trairūpya* on the grounds (1) that it seems to insist on the necessity both of affirmative instances, XP, and of negative instances, X-non-P, although as a matter of fact there are valid types of argument which are either purely positive (*kevalānvayin*), no negative instances being available, or purely negative (*kevalavyatirekin*), no positive instances being available (pp. 24-25); (2) that it is necessary to insert restrictive phrases

[1] *asat* is usually interpreted as =*asiddha*, the 'unreal' reason which is not in fact found in S. So Keith, *ILA*, p. 133, following what appears to be Praśastapāda's interpretation of the *sūtra*. But Praśastapāda is really reading two classes—*asiddha* and *viruddha*—into the one rubric, *asat*, of the *sūtra*. The example given by the *sūtra*—"this is a horse because it has horns"—is almost certainly intended as an example of a middle which proves the contradictory (*viruddha*): though of course horses have no horns, and therefore the example would also exemplify *asiddha*. It seems to me that the conception of *asiddha* is a relatively late addition to the classification of fallacies. The *saṁdigdha* and the *viruddha* of course break the second and third canons respectively—presence *only* in the *sapakṣa*, and absence in the *vipakṣa*.

in each canon—S is *only* M (=*All* S is M); *only* XP is M (=*All* M is P); M is *only-not* X-non-P (=M never is non-P)—in order to exclude the cases of illicit minor (*asiddha*) and undistributed middle or illicit major (*saṁdigdha*). But if we do this the second or the third canon is otiose, since both mean the same thing; and the second canon contradicts the first, since to say that *only* XP is M implies that S is *not* M.[1] Uddyotakara's criticism seems to be justified, since the introduction of the doctrine of *vyāpti* had in fact profoundly modified the older view of inference as an affair of example; and the *trairūpya* is really a statement of the canons of the older or paradeigmatic syllogism.

Formal logic of the syllogism.

Fragment J.

A formal syllogistic was developed, perhaps by Diṅnāga, out of the *trairūpya*. The *hetu-cakra*, or scheme of Nine Reasons, ignores the relation of M to S (the first canon, which serves to exclude *asiddha* fallacies), and distinguishes nine types of argument on the basis of the relation of the middle term to the *sapakṣa* XP and the *vipakṣa* X-non-P—that is, on the basis of the second and third canons. The middle term may reside in all, or some only, or in none of the cases of P (*sapakṣa-vyāpaka*, *sapakṣaikadeśavṛtti*, *sapakṣāvṛtti*); and similarly in all, some, or no non-P (*vipakṣavyāpaka*, *vipakṣaikadeśavṛtti*, *vipakṣāvṛtti*). Two types are valid (*sapakṣavyā-*

[1] This is the criticism which Dharmakīrti attempted to meet by the doctrine of aggregative restriction (see pp. 16-17), maintaining that the second canon should be taken to mean "only XP *and* S are M." But the truth is that the *trairūpya* cannot be patched up to fit the view of inference as an affair of connections between abstract P and M, being essentially a formulation of the paradeigmatic syllogism, which is concerned with concrete SP and XP, and not with abstract P. So that Uddyotakara's criticism is substantially just. And, with regard to the first canon, Diṅnāga seems to have left the meaning of *anumeya* ambiguous. It might mean P in the abstract; in which case Uddyotakara's objection that there is no statement of the requirement that S must be M will be justified; and further, the second and third canons become otiose, since the first one states that All M is P. And if it means S, then there will be in the *trairūpya* no statement of the *vyāpti* between P and M, since the second and third canons are concerned with concrete XP, and not with abstract P.

paka-vipakṣāvṛtti, and *sapakṣaikadeśavṛtti-vipakṣāvṛtti*); two are contradictory or *viruddha* (*sapakṣāvṛtti-vipakṣavyāpaka*, and *sapakṣāvṛtti-vipakṣaikadeśavṛtti*); the other five are inconclusive or *aniścita*, though one of them (*sapakṣāvṛtti-vipakṣāvṛtti*, where M is a peculiar property of P, so that neither positive nor negative instances are forthcoming) holds a special position and is called *asādhāraṇa*.[1] Uddyotakara argues in the first place that an *asādhāraṇa-dharma* or peculiar property of S may be a valid reason if there *are* no instances of non-P; and he points out in the second place that the example which the *Bauddha* gives of a valid reason, "Sound is non-eternal, because a product," would be purely positive (*kevalānvayin*) on the Buddhist view that there is nothing eternal: so that the *Bauddha* ought to provide a place for valid purely positive arguments,[2] but fails to do so.

Note to Fragment H. The other scheme, of Seven Types (p. 24), ignores the minor details of the *hetu-cakra*, but takes into account the relation of M to S, *i.e.* the first canon, thus arriving at the conception of the reason with three characteristics (*trilakṣaṇa-hetu*) as alone valid: those which have only one or two of the characters being (i) unreal (*asiddha*), (ii) inconclusive (*saṁdigdha*), or (iii) contradictory (*viruddha*). Uddyotakara repeats the criticism that some of the arguments which have

[1] Uddyotakara draws a necessary distinction between the case where there *is no* evidence (*avidyamānasapakṣa, avidyamānavipakṣa*) and the cases where there *are* instances of P or of non-P, and M is not found in these instances (*sapakṣāvṛtti, vipakṣāvṛtti*). On the basis of this distinction he is able to recognise as valid the purely positive argument or *kevalānvayin* (*avidyamānavipakṣa-sapakṣavyāpaka*), and the purely negative argument (*avidyamānasapakṣa-vipakṣāvṛtti*) such as "the organism is endowed with a soul because it has vital functions." This latter, which was subsequently called the *kevalavyatirekin*, he sometimes denominates the *avīta-hetu*, sometimes simply *vyatirekin*, and definitely asserts its validity. As regards the purely positive type see next note.

[2] It is not clear whether Uddyotakara himself admits the validity of the purely positive argument, as the later *Nyāya* school does. He never gives an example of such an argument which he would himself admit as valid; and his argument in favour of it never goes beyond the *argumentum ad hominem* that the *Bauddha* would have admitted it if he had been consistent with himself.

only two of the characters (*i.e.*, satisfy either the second or the third canon, but not both) are either valid purely negative arguments, or are given by the *Bauddha* himself as examples of valid arguments, although on his own theories they should belong to the purely positive type.

Fallacies.

Besides fallacies of the middle term, Diṅnāga, like Praśastapāda, recognised fallacies of the Exemplification or major premise (*udāharaṇābhāsa*), which speaking very roughly might be equated with 'inductive fallacies'; and fallacies of the thesis or Proposition.

1. Fallacies of the middle term include, besides the unreal, the inconclusive, and the contradictory reasons connected with the formal syllogistic outlined in the preceding paragraphs, the case of antinomy or antinomic reason (*viruddhāvyabhicārin*). An antinomy would exist where two otherwise valid reasons led to contradictory conclusions. This conception was accepted by the later *Nyāya* school, under the title of *satpratipakṣa;* but Praśastapāda rejects Diṅnāga's doctrine, arguing that either one of the reasons is less cogent than the other, in which case the thesis supported by the less cogent reason should be classed as a fallacious thesis;[1] or else the *co-existence* in the Subject of a pair of properties, which, taken alone, lead to contradictory conclusions, is a peculiar property (*asādhāraṇa*) of the subject in question, in which case it falls under his rubric of *anadhyavasita*, an appearance of reason which really leads to no conclusion at all. For Praśastapāda rejects Diṅnāga's classification of the *asādhāraṇa* as a species of inconclusive argument (*saṁdigdha*, *aniścita*), on the ground that a doubtful reason is one in which there is *some* evidence though the evidence is inconclusive; whereas in the case of an *asādhāraṇa-dharma* or peculiar property there are from the

1. *Hetvābhāsa.*

The antinomy: see pp. 68-69.

Praśastapāda's criticism of Diṅnāga's treatment of the *asādhāraṇa* fallacy.

[1] He uses the word *viruddha* of such a reason—which does not mean the *viruddha-hetvābhāsa*, but stands for *viruddha* as used in the names of the varieties of *pratijñābhāsa*.

nature of the case no similar cases, and therefore *no* evidence at all; and mere absence of evidence is not a ground of doubt (*saṁdehakāraṇa*), but leads to no conclusion at all (*adhyavasāyaṁ na karoti*)—not even to an inconclusive conclusion.

Fragment K. The *asiddha*.

One fragment (pp. 34-36) indicates some doubt on Diṅnāga's part as to the nature and reality of the *asiddha* fallacy. There is no doubt that he did class it as one of the fallacies of the middle term (*hetvābhāsa*). His scheme of Seven Types referred to above would suffice to prove this, and Sugiura states explicitly that he did so in the *Nyāya-dvāra*. But here we find him saying that valid and fallacious middles are alike *pakṣadharma*, resident in S,—which accords with his ignoring of the first canon in his scheme of Nine Types.

2. *Pratijñābhāsa* and the *bādhita-hetvābhāsa*.

2. Fallacies of the thesis correspond to the *bādhita* fallacy of the classical *Nyāya*, which held that the valid reason must be possessed not only of the three characters formulated in the *trairūpya*, but also of two further characters—it must not be *satpratipakṣa*, or antinomised, and it must not be *bādhita*, or annulled by prior knowledge. The valid reason is therefore described as *pañcarūpopapanna*, possessed of five characters. Details of the fallacies of thesis have been given at pp. 62-64, *supra*. The conception of a fallacious thesis is open to logical objection, since the argument in support of a thesis which is 'annulled' by facts cannot satisfy the canons of syllogism, and will be reducible to one of the fallacies of middle term. But the practical convenience of at once cutting short an opponent who propounds an absurdity is obvious; and in dealing with an opponent who is prepared to maintain that black is white, or that the law of contradiction does not hold, there is really no other course open. He puts himself out of court at once.

3. *Udāharaṇābhāsa*.

3. Fallacies of exemplification disappear from later logic, their place being taken by the extended meaning given to the *asiddha* or unreal reason, a name which was ultimately applied, not merely to a middle term which does not reside in S, but also to one which is not proved by the examples adduced to be

inseparably connected with P. The ambiguity of the term *anumeya*, which meant either S or P or both at once (S qualified by P, SP), gave a very elastic character, at first to the first canon of the *trairūpya*,[1] and subsequently perhaps to the fallacy—*asiddha*—which that canon was meant to exclude. The process by which the Fallacies of Exemplification were absorbed later into the ill-conceived rubric of *asiddha* was perhaps facilitated by the fact (referred to at p. 70, *supra*) that Praśastapāda used the same names for certain varieties of *udāharaṇābhāsa* which he had already used for certain varieties of *asiddha-hetvābhāsa*.

A *fallacy of exemplification* is committed when the example adduced does not show concomitance between M and P, or does not prove a *universal* connection between them in the form All M is P. This corresponds to the *vyāpyatvāsiddha* of the later schools (Keith, *ILA*, p. 145). *An unreal reason*, for Diṅnāga and Praśastapāda, is a property (i) the *residence* of which in the Subject is denied by both parties; or is (ii) controversial; or (iii) the *character* of which is doubtful (as when what we see in the distance may be either vapour or smoke); or (iv) which is attributed to a subject which is unreal in that connection (as when we argue that darkness is a substance because it has qualities—the fact being that darkness is unreal in any sense which would admit of the attribution of qualities to it as their possessor).[2]

[1] The confusion as to the meaning of the first canon is very plain in Praśastapāda and Diṅnāga, and the reason why we cannot define just what they meant by it is simply that they did not know themselves. See the discussion in Keith's *ILA*, pp. 137, 140. I do not think that there is any difference between the senses in which Praśastapāda and Diṅnāga interpreted the first canon. The meaning of it is equally indeterminate for either.

[2] The names of these varieties in Praśastapāda are *ubhayāsiddha*, *anyatarāsiddha*, *svabhāvāsiddha*, and *anumeyāsiddha*. Cf. *HIL*, p. 293.

As names of fallacies of exemplification *ubhayāsiddha* means that the example adduced possesses neither M nor P, while *anumeyāsiddha* means that it does not possess P.

'*Inference for Another.*'

It was characteristic of *Vaiśeṣika-Bauddha* logic to draw sharply the distinction, which had not been made clear in the *Nyāya Sūtra* and *Bhāṣya*, between inference as a mental process (*svārthānumāna*),[1] and inference expressed in words (*parārthānumāna*, 'inference for another'). The drawing of this distinction was an inevitable step in the progressive clearing up of logical conceptions; but it has been suggested that it is connected with the rejection by the Buddhist of 'word' or testimony as a separate source of knowledge.[2] Inference as a mental process involves only two elements or premises: observation of the middle or mark (*liṅga-darśana*), and remembrance of the universal connection between the mark and the property to be proved (*vyāpti-smaraṇa*). When expressed in words for the information of others, a syllogism has five members according to the *Nyāya* and *Vaiśeṣika* schools—hence its name, *pañcāvayavavākya*. But the *Bauddha* seems to have regarded two of the 'members' as superfluous, namely the *upanaya*, or application, and the *nigamana*, or conclusion.

Fragment I (1).

The *Nyāya Sūtra* defines the other three members in a manner which laid it open to the criticisms of Vasubandhu, as confusing the mental process of inference with the statements (*vākya*) in which it finds expression. Thus the Proposition is defined as "the statement of the *probandum*" (*sādhya-nirdeśaḥ pratijñā*); the Reason, as "the means of proving the *probandum* from likeness to the example" (*udāharaṇa-sādharmyāt sādhya-sādhanaṁ hetuḥ*); and the Example or Exemplification, as "an accepted case which has the *probandum*-property as the result of a property in which it resembles the Subject of the

Definition of the 'members' of the syllogism in the *Nyāya Sūtra*.

[1] Usually translated 'inference for oneself.' But it is doubtful whether *-artha* in this compound has the meaning 'for the sake of,' since Praśastapāda uses the term *sva-niścitārthānumāna*, which would mean inference of a thing ascertained by oneself.

[2] Keith, *ILA*, p. 107.

inference" (*sādhya-sādharmyāt tad*[1]*-dharma-bhāvī dṛṣṭānta udāharaṇam*). It is clear that the first is a definition of a premise expressed in words, while the other two are definitions of inferential functions as such; and from this point of view Vasubandhu is justified in saying the three members are badly formulated (*trayo 'vayavā durvihitāḥ*, p. 25) in Akṣapāda's definition. The *Bauddha* himself gives separate definitions of the *probandum* as such (*pakṣa*) and of the statement of the *probandum* (*pratijñā*; see footnote to p. 27). Diṅnāga follows the line taken up by Vasubandhu in his criticism of the definition of the Reason (pp. 43-45).

Vasubandhu's criticism. Section 13.

Diṅnāga's criticism. Fragment L.

Validity.

The problem of the validity of knowledge took in the Indian schools the form of asking whether the validity and invalidity (*prāmāṇya*, *aprāmāṇya*) of cognition is apprehended from the cognition itself (*svataḥ*) or from some extrinsic source (*parataḥ*). The schools are classified according to their answer to this question in some well-known lines cited in the *Tārkika-rakṣā* of Varada Rāja, from which we learn that the *Bauddhas* held that invalidity is intrinsic to a cognition as such, validity extrinsic to it. The great difficulty on the *Bauddha's* view is, in fact, to explain how cognition can ever be valid. He is represented (p. 29) as arguing that it does not matter whether he himself accepts the validity of the reasoning process or not, provided that he can refute his opponents with weapons which they themselves accept. This is, however, a position which it is impossible to maintain consistently, and the *Bauddha's* opponents point out that he himself inconsistently defines proof as "a reason accepted by *both* parties to a discussion," and inference for another as "setting forth a conclusion which one has seen for oneself." If the *Bauddha* accepts no reason,

Fragment I (ii). Fragment I (i).

[1] Vātsyāyana points out that *tad* stands for *sādhya*, and that *sādhya* now means *sādhya-dharmin*, S, whereas in *sādhya-sādharmyāt* it means *sādhya-dharma*, P—an interesting example of the ambiguity of the term. (*NBh*, p. 41 [on *NS*, I, i, 36].)

he can never (on his own definition) prove anything (pp. 23 and 53); nor can he ever set forth in words a syllogism for the instruction of others, since he can never have seen the force of an inference himself. His definition of Discussion (*vāda*) as "statement to prove one's own position and to disprove the opponent's" will be similarly open to objection: though as a matter of fact Uddyotakara criticises it on other grounds (pp. 39 and 55).

Fragment P.

Fragment O.

Diṅnāga himself, in a much-quoted fragment, says that inference can have no reference to (ultimate) reality and non-reality, seeing that the function of inference turns wholly on the distinction of subject and predicate, a distinction which is illusorily imposed on reality by thought (pp. 51-52). To the objection that, if inference is unreal, the Buddhist cannot consistently use it for his own purposes, the reply is that inference has just as much reality as the ideal construction to which alone it applies—the whole business of knowledge and its objects is on the phenomenal plane (*samvṛti*, p. 53).

So far as inference is concerned, then, Diṅnāga is a thorough-going idealist. It is only in his doctrine of pure perception, as somehow putting us in touch with the unique moments of existence which constitute the ultimate reality, that realistic tendencies show themselves in his logic. When we have removed all the ideal elements which overlay the pure percept and constitute what is ordinarily called perception, *something* still remains. But, of course, about this 'something' nothing at all can be said. It is, as Uddyotakara puts it, "like a dumb man's dream."[1]

[1] *mūka-svapna-vat:* which is equivalent, as noted by Keith, to the modern philosopher's remark that a consistent sensationalist should be speechless.

INDEX

I. ENGLISH

II. SANSKRIT